To

CHARLES LOUIS BOOTH

My 90 year old father, whose
interest is unfailing and
always encouraging.

<u>CHARLES CITY</u>
1634

Prince George
1703

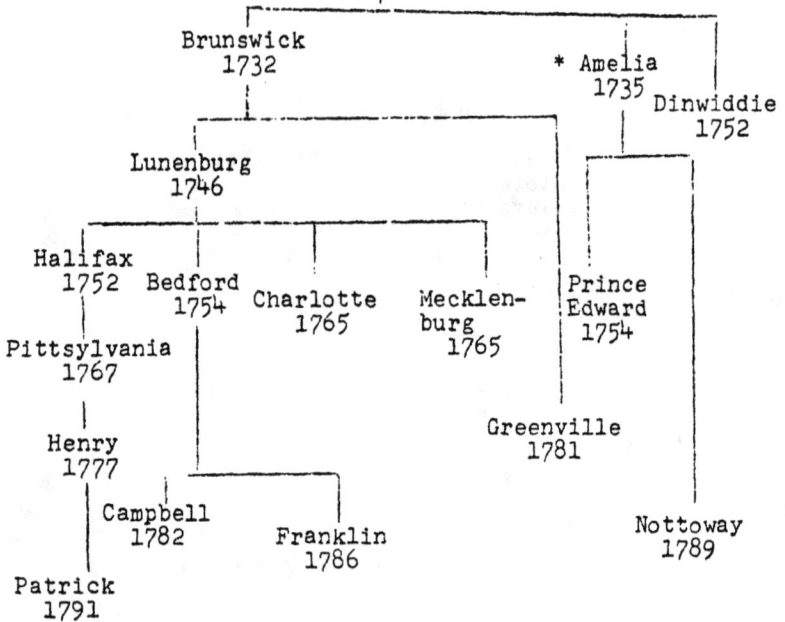

Brunswick
1732

* Amelia
1735

Dinwiddie
1752

Lunenburg
1746

Halifax
1752

Bedford
1754

Charlotte
1765

Mecklen-
burg
1765

Prince
Edward
1754

Pittsylvania
1767

Greenville
1781

Henry
1777

Campbell
1782

Franklin
1786

Nottoway
1789

Patrick
1791

* Initially formed from more
than one county.

From:
Robinson's History of
Virginia Counties,
p. 164

MARRIAGES

of

AMELIA COUNTY

VIRGINIA

1735-1815

Compiled by

KATHLEEN BOOTH WILLIAMS

CLEARFIELD

Reprinted for
Clearfield Company, Inc. by
Genealogical Publishing Co., Inc.
Baltimore, Maryland
1992, 1996, 2000, 2005

Originally published: Alexandria, Virginia, 1961
Reprinted from a volume in the library of
The Maryland Historical Society
Baltimore, Maryland, by
Genealogical Publishing Co., Inc.
Baltimore, 1979
© 1961 Kathleen Booth Williams
© transferred to Genealogical Publishing Co., Inc.
Baltimore, Maryland, 1978
All Rights Reserved
Library of Congress Catalogue Card Number 78-65699
International Standard Book Number 0-8063-0835-4
Made in the United States of America

FOREWORD

Amelia, named for the Princess Amelia (Sophia),
youngest daughter of King George II of England, was formed
from Prince George and Brunswick in 1735 (1734). (A Horn-
book of Virginia, p. 11.)

At a meeting of the General Assembly on August 8,
1734, an Act was passed for the formation of Amelia County and reads in part:
> That from and immediately after the twenty
> fifth day of March, now next ensuing, the
> said county of Prince George, and that
> part of the parish of Bristol which lies
> in the same, be divided, from the mouth
> of Namozain creek, up the same, to the
> main, or John Hamlin's fork of the said
> creek; thence up the south or lowest
> branch thereof, to White-Oak Hunting Path;
> and thence, by a south course, to strike
> Nottoway river: And that all of that part
> of the said county, below those courses,
> be thereafter one distinct county, and
> retain the name of Prince George county:
> And all that territory of land, above
> the said courses, bounded southerly by
> Great Nottoway river, including part of
> the county of Brunswick, and parish of
> St. Andrew, so far as to take the ridges
> between Roanoak and Appomatox rivers;
> and thence, along those ridges, to the
> great mountains, westerly by the said
> mountains, and northerly by the southern
> boundaries of Goochland and Henrico
> counties, be thence erected into one
> other distinct county and parish, and
> called and known by the name of Amelia
> County, and Raleigh parish.

The Act also provides that the vestrymen living on
each side of this line be vestrymen of the respective
parish in his county; and that to complete the number
of vestrymen needed in each parish, the people living
in each area should meet and "elect and choose" enough
men to meet the need. (Henning 4, pp. 467, 468).

When Amelia was first formed, it contained what is
now Prince Edward and Nottoway Counties.

October 1748 - 22^d George II
Private Acts
64. -   An Act for dividing the Parish of Raleigh,
          in the county of Amelia, and erecting the
          same into two distinct parishes. (Henning
          6, p. 211).
          (Nottoway Parish?) (This is all that is
          given.).

     At a meeting of the General Assembly on May 28,
1755, an Act was passed for the division of Nottoway
Parish and the formation of St. Patrick's Parish "on
the first day of September next." St. Patrick's Parish
fell into Prince Edward county when it was taken from
Amelia in 1754 (1753).

     Nottoway Parish was left in Amelia until Nottoway
county was separated from Amelia in 1789 (1788).

     For these marriages, the Register, Index to Mar-
riage Bonds, was copied at the Clerk's Office at Amelia;
then, as many original bonds, consents and Ministers'
Returns as one may consult were checked.

     There are two drawers of records closed to the
public by Order of the Court because they are so
fragile. The bonds in these drawers were copied by
the Clerk, each on a separate sheet of paper and each
is signed by him. They give the name of groom, name of
bride, date and surety. The bonds at Amelia, except a
very few, give no witnesses other than a Court Official.
Hence, when consents show witnesses, I have included
their names. Also included are marriages shown in Ministers' Returns for which no bonds were found.

     The first part of the above Register was compiled by
Mr. Stephen L. Farrar, Sr., "who was Judge of Amelia County from 1898 to 1907, at which time the County Court was
abolished, by law, and most of its functions assumed by
the Circuit Court. The same year Mr. Farrar was appoint-
ed County Clerk and Clerk of the Circuit Court of
Amelia. It was during the following years he compiled
the Register."
(The above quotation is from information written about
his father by Mr. Stephen L. Farrar, Jr., the present
Clerk of the Court of Amelia.)

     The first part of the Register is written in Mr.
Farrar's own handwriting. Where he left off, his son
took up the work, and the part done by Mr. Farrar, Jr.
is typed into the Register. The Register gives marriages through 1950.

Ministers' Returns were made by:

Charles Anderson - Baptist
John Brunskill
James Burkes
James Chappell
William Dier (Dyer) (he
    signed both ways)
Joseph Finnell
John Finney - Methodist
Charles Forsee - Baptist
Edmund Goode
John Goode
Thomas Grymes
Devereux Jarratt
David Jones - Methodist
John Jones - Methodist
Walthall Robertson -
                Baptist
Chas. Roper
Samuel Rucker
John Skurrey (Scurry,
    Scurrie) - Baptist
Conrad Speece
Edmund Talley

Elkanah Talley - Episcopal
John King
Drury Lang
Zachariah G. Leigh -Baptist
James McGlasson
Robert Marshall
Bennett Maxey
Thomas Pettus
Winson (?) H. Pitman
John Pollard - Baptist
John H. Rice
Arch. W. Roberts
George Robertson
Milton Robertson -
            Christian Church
Jesse Talley
David Thomson
Jeremiah Walker - Separate
                Baptist
Robert Walthall -Methodist
Simeon Walton
Abner Watkins
H. Wood, L. M. M. E. C.

I extend to Mr. Stephen L. Farrar, Jr., Clerk; Judge
Valentine Southall; and Mrs. G. M. Shanks, Deputy Clerk,
sincere gratitude for their courtesy, their help and for
treating me as an honored guest during the weeks I
worked at Amelia Court House.

I thank Miss Eula Haskew, of Brownwood, Texas, for
voluntarily sending information, with reference to
proof, as to who Sarah Esken (Haskew?), was. (p. 77,
this book.).

Kathleen Booth Williams.

MARRIAGES OF AMELIA COUNTY, VIRGINIA

1735 - 1815

-- ----- ----. ABNEY, Dennit and ---- -----. Sur. Thomas Burton. (Parent or Guardian - bond mutilated.) Wit. Sam'l Cobbs and John Neve. p. A-1

12 December 1785. ADAMS, Dancy and Dolcy Clay. Sur. John Clay. p. A-1

24 April 1788. ADAMS, Dancy and Nancy Farley. Sur. Mathew Farley. p. A-1

13 December 1802. ADDAMS, Dancy and Patsey Cardwell, dau. of Richard Cardwell, who consents. Wit. to consent, Joseph Cook and Stephen Spain. Sur. Joseph Cook. p. A-2

1 April 1782. ADAMS, David and Rachel Coleman. Sur. Burwell Coleman. p. A-1

16 August 1790. ADAMS, David and Dolly Tanner. Sur. Robert Tanner. Married 21 August by Rev. Walthall Robertson. p. A-1

18 April 1795. ADAMS, David and Lucy Ragland. Married 18 April by Rev. Walthall Robertson. Minister's Return.

26 December 1809. ADAMS, John and Elizabeth R. Clay, spinster, dau. of Charles Clay, Sr., who consents. Wit. to consent, Wm. Curry and Jesse Clay. Sur. Wm. C. Avery. p. A-2

13 April 1795. ADAMS, William and Jincey Ragland. Sur. Jeremiah Tanner. p. A-2

18 March 1801. ADAMS, Wylie and Sally Young, who writes her own consent. Wit. to consent, A. Tucker and Bartlet Walthal. Sur. Anderson Tucker. p. A-2

28 November 1787. ADSON, Charles and Fanny Riddle. Sur. Samuel Bentley. p. A-1

28 September 1814. ALLEN, Alexander and Martha Allen, dau. of William Allen, who consents. Wit. to consent, Sherman Woodward and Armistead Coleman. Sur. Armistead Coleman. Married 30 September by Rev. James Chappell. p. A-3

4 December 1809. ALLEN, Benjamin, Jr. and Jane Jeter, dau
of Rodophil Jeter, who consents and says Jane is under age.
Wit. to consent, Anthony Crenshaw. Sur. James Gills. Married 8 December by Rev. Conrad Speece. p. A-2

4 September 1758. ALLEN, Daniel and Frances Neal, who
writes her own consent. Sur. John Haskinson. p. A-1

10 April 1790. ALLEN, Daniel and Tabitha Coleman, dau. of
Jesse and Sarah Coleman, who consent. Sur. Arahart Crowder. p. A-1

25 December 1806. ALLEN, Daniel and Sarah Clay. Sur. John
Allen. p. A-2

24 September ----. ALLEN, James and Susannah Bevill.
Daniel Allen's consent, 23 September, says: "let James
Allen marry my daughter, Suzaner Bevill." Consent also
signed by Lucy Bevill. Sur. Richard Allen. Rev. C. H.
Roper certifies they were married 17 October 1801.
(This marriage is not in the Register.)

17 March 1806. ALLEN, James and Elizabeth Jeter, dau. of
Rodophil Jeter, who consents. Wit. to consent, Jane Jeter
and James Gills. Sur. James Gills. Married 18 March by
Rev. Drury Lang (?). p. A-2

15 August 1807. ALLEN, James and Davis Pollard, dau. of
George Pollard, who consents. Wit. to consent, Joseph
Pollard. Sur. Joseph Pollard. (The Register says Rodophil
Jeter gives this consent - consent says George Pollard,
who says, "my daughter." p. A-2

27 August 1802. ALLEN, John and Nancy Hill Bevill, who
writes her own consent. Wit. to consent, James Allen and
Daniel Allen. Sur. James Allen. p. A-2

30 July 1779. ALLEN, Richard and Winefred Vaughan, widow.
Sur. William Allen of Dinwiddie County. Richard Allen is
of Dinwiddie County. p. A-1

26 January 1792. ALLEN, Richard and Elizabeth Tabbitt (?)
Phillips. Both are of Amelia County. Sur. Barney
Phillips. p. A-2

21 January 1812. ALLEN, Richard and Tabitha Southall, dau.
of John Southall, who consents. Wit. to consent, Barnett
Southall, Henry Southall and Jesse Southall. Sur. Barnett
Southall. Married 24 January by Rev. Richard Allen.
p. A-2 (See Richard Allen.)

24 January 1812. ALLEN, Richard and Tabitha Coleman.
Married by Rev. James Chappell. See Richard Allen.
Minister's Return.

16 March 1784. ALLEN, William and Betsy Johnson. Sur.
Archer Johnson. p. A-1

4 October 1804. ALLEN, William and Polly W. Deaton. Sur.
John Deaton. Married 6 October by Rev. John Skurrey.
p. A-2

24 June 1780. ALLFRIEND, Benjamin and Ann Dudley, dau. of
Edward W. Dudley, who consents. Wit. to consent, Isham
Malone and James Dudley. Sur. Samuel Morgan. p. A-1

15 May 1809 (07?). AMBLER, Edward and Sarah Taylor Holcombe. Phil Holcombe, her Guardian, consents 15 May
1807 (09?). Wit. to consent, Wal. Holcombe and Barret
Burton. Sur. Barret Burton. p. A-2

20 December 1805. ANDERSON, Charles and Fanny Ponton,
who writes her own consent. Wit. to consent, Thomas M.
Cobbs. Sur. Thomas M. Cobbs. p. A-2

27 March 1800. ANDERSON, Churchill and Polly Goode. Her
Guardian, Parham Booker, consents. Wit. to consent, Wal-
ler Ford. Sur. Waller Ford. Married 3 April by Rev.
David Thomson. p. A-2

13 July 1801. ANDERSON, Claiborne and Polly Branch Jones.
Chamberlain Jones consents. Wit. to consent, Daniel Willson and John Sudbury. Sur. Daniel Willson, Sr. p. A-2

9 July 1742. ANDERSON, Francis and Edith Weldon. Sur.
James Scott. Wit. to bond, Sam'l Cobbs. p. A-1

1 May 1790. ANDERSON, Francis and Sally Anderson Blackburn. Sur. Harry Gaines. p. A-1

24 July 1760. ANDERSON, Henry and Martha Cocke. Henry
Anderson, her Guardian, consents. Wit. to consent, Rolf
Eldridge and Gray Briggs. Sur. Ben Ward. p. A-1

26 September 1783. ANDERSON, James and Sally Bagley,
dau. of George Bagley, who consents. Wit. to consent,
Henry Anderson and Wm. Beanttry (?). Sur. Peter Randolph. Married 1 October by Rev. Charles Anderson.
p. A-1

30 November 1812. ANDERSON, James P. and Martha L. Hutcherson. John Jones, Sr. consents. Sur. William Hutcherson. Married 5 December by Rev. Zachariah G. Leigh. p. A-3

17 May 1787. ANDERSON, Matthew and Martha Disen. Martha Disen consents and says Martha is of age. Wit. to consent, John Walton and Stokes Anderson. Sur. John Walton. p. A-1

9 April 1789. ANDERSON, Mathew and Polly Bagley. George Bagley consents. Wit. to consent, James Bagley and Jno. Bagley. Sur. James Bagley. p. A-1

15 December 1784. ANDERSON, Reinard and Mary Ford. Sur. Edwd H. Toms. p. A-1

4 March 1761. ANDERSON, Richard and Jane Foster. Sur. Thomas Foster. p. A-1

17 November 1784. ANDERSON, Worsham and Misaniah Knight, dau. of Charles Knight, who consents. Wit. to consent, Coleman Knight and John Tabb. Sur. John Tabb. p. A-1

21 April 1783. ANDREWS, Knacy and Lucy Green, dau. of Lucy Green, who consents. Wit. to consent, John Green and George Green. Sur. George Green. Knacy Andrews is of Mecklenburg County. p. A-1

26 February 1784. ANGELL, John and Elizabeth Hundley. Sur. John Hundley. p. A-1

20 October 1808. ANGEL, John D. and Polly T. Roberts, dau. of Jacob Roberts, who consents. Sur. Jacob Roberts. Married 27 October by Rev. John Skurrey. p. A-2

25 December 1812. ANGEL, Robert J. and Judith Roberts, dau. of Jacob Roberts, who consents. Wit. to consent, William W. Osborne and Wm. H. Vaughan. Sur. William W. Osborne. Married 26 December by Rev. John Skurrey. p. A-2

22 February 1776. ARCHER, Henry and Mary Randolph. Both are of Raleigh Parish. Sur. Sam'l. Sherwin. p. A-1

7 December 1768. ARCHER, John and Anne Hall, who writes her own consent. Wit. to consent, Fanny Hall. Sur. Thomas Hall. p. A-1

4 December 1784. ARCHER, John and Ann Bott. Sur. Joel Bott. p. A-1

24 April 1788. ARCHER, John and Elizabeth Eggleston. Sur. Is. Holmes. (In top of bond is Isaac Holmes.) p. A-1

8 February 1760. ARCHER, John and Elizabeth Townes,
widow, who writes her own consent. Sur. Wm. ___let.
John Archer is of Chesterfield County. p. A-1

17 February 1801. ARCHER, John R. and Frances C. Tabb,
dau. of Frances Tabb, who consents and says Dr. John R.
Archer. Wit. to consent, Bathurst Randolph and Mary Randolph. Sur. Bathurst Randolph. p. A-2

8 October 1810. ARCHER, Miles and Nancy W. Archer, dau.
of William Archer, who consents. Wit. to consent,
Instance Hall and Elizabeth Archer. Sur. Instance Hall.
Married 9 October by Rev. Zachariah G. Leigh. p. A-2

22 October 1782. ARCHER, Peter F. and Frances Tanner, dau.
of Branch Tanner, whose consent says, Peter Field Archer.
Wit. to consent, W. B. Willson and John Truly. Sur. Ludwell Brackett. p. A-1

22 January 1799. ARCHER, Peter Field and Judith E. Cocke.
Sur. John Booker, Jr. p. A-2

8 September 1812. ARCHER, Peterfield and Ann Jones.
John Jones, Senr. consents. Wit. to consent, Peter Jones
and Wood Jones. Sur. Peter Jones. p. A-3

14 June 1794. ARCHER, Richard and Mary Chastain Cocke.
Sur. Stephen Cocke. Married 19 June by Rev. Elkanah Talley, Protestant Episcopal. p. A-2

3 March 1791. ARCHER, William and Prudence Callicott,
dau. of James Callicoate, who consents. Wit. to consent,
John L. Cooper and John Archer. Sur. John L. Cooper.
Married by Rev. John Brunskill. p. A-2

24 June 1791. ASSELIN, Francis and Edith Cobbs, who
writes her own consent. Wit. to consent, Jesse Hillsman
and John E. Cobbs. Sur. Thomas Morris. Married by Rev.
John Brunskill. p. A-2

23 December 1800. ATKINSON, Jeremiah and Betsy Meadows.
Sur. Thomas Meador. Married by Rev. John Pollard. p. A-2

6 December 1759. ATWOOD, James and Mary Turner, widow.
Sur. Henry Ward. p. A-1

19 February 1801. AVERY, Joel and Sally Ellington. Sur.
John Madderra. p. A-2

24 October 1795. AVARY, Nathan and Elizabeth Williams,
dau. of Philip Williams, whose consent says Nathan Avery.
Wit. to consent, Edward Atkinson and James Atkinson.
Sur. James Atkinson. p. A-2

20 November 1809. AVERY, William C. and Dolly Clay, dau. of Charles Clay. Sur. Charles Clay. p. A-2

20 December 1814. AYRES, Joseph W. and Mary Booker Overton, dau. of Mary Overton, who consents. Wit. to consent, Parham Booker and John Brazeal. Sur. John H. Brazeal. p. A-3

8 April 1789. BAGLEY, James and Rachel Crenshaw, dau. of James Crenshaw, who consents. Wit. to consent, Matthew Anderson and Robert Crenshaw. This is consent only. See Js. Bagley (Bayley?).

9 April 1789. BAGLEY (Bayley?), Js. and Rosa Crenshaw. Sur. Mathew Anderson. See James Bagley. (Bond badly mutilated.) p. B-4

28 November 1799. BAILEY, Jeremiah and Frances R. Cousins. Sur. John C. Cousins. p. B-5

20 June 1766. BAILEY, John and Mary Metcalf Sallard. Both of Nottoway Parish, Amelia County. Sur. Chas. Sallard. P. B-1

27 August 1761. BAINES, Francis and Ann Brackett. Sur. Thomas Brackett. p. B-1

24 May 1784. BAKER, John and Frances Walthall. Sur. Alex'r. Walker. p. B-3

-- July 176-. BAKER, Sam'l and (mutilated). Sur. _____. In Presence of Jno. Vas___ and Abrm. _____. p. B-1

30 October 1800. BALDWIN, Geo. W. and Elizabeth Vaughan, dau. of Nicholas Vaughan, who consents. Wit. to consent, Willis Vaughan and James Townes, C. A. C. Sur. Willis Vaughan. Married 4 November by Rev. John Skurrey. p. B-6

13 August 1778. BALDWIN, John, Jr. and Mary Angell. Sur. James Cooke. p. B-2

-- ----- ----. BALDWIN, Samuel and Mary Griffin. Married by Rev. Charles Anderson. Returned 24 August 1786.

26 March 1801. BALDWIN, William A. and Nancy Williams, dau. of Philip Williams, who consents on 25 March. Wit. to consent, Joseph Mottley and Booker Foster. Sur. Joseph Mottley. Married 31 March by Rev. John Skurrey. p. B-6

14 July 1811. BALL, Isham and Jane Morris. Joseph Morris consents. Sur. Jos. Hobson. p. B-7

4 February 1755. BANISTER, John and Elizabeth Munford.
Sur. Edward Jones. p. B-1

21 December 1807. BANISTER, Theodoric B. and Seigniora
Tabb, who writes her own consent. She is dau. of Frances
Tabb, who consents also and says, "my daughter to Theod-
eric Blair Bannister." Sur. John R. Archer. p. B-6

14 January 1801. BANNISTER, Tinsley and Milley Shore.
Married 14 January by Rev. John Pollard. Minister's
Return.

11 February 1814. BARDING, Davis and Rachel Barding.
Sur. William Barding. Wit. to bond, Benjn. Lawson. See
Lewis Barding. p. B-7

28 March 1815. BARDING, John and Catharine Sadler, dau.
of Sam Sadler, who consents. Wit. to consent, Mordecai
Perrin. Sur. Mordecai Perrin. Married 29 May by Rev.
John Skurrey. p. B-7

10 February 1814. BARDING, Lewis and Rachel Barding.
Married by Rev. John Skurrey. Minister's Return. See
Davis Barding.

23 August 1787. BARDING, William and Oney Wingo, who
writes her own consent. Wit. to consent, Matthew Seay
and Abraham Seay. Sur. Gideon Seay. p. B-3

31 May 1815. BARKSDALE, William I. and Marianna E. Tabb,
dau. of Frances Tabb, who consents. Wit. to consent, W.
W. Banister and T. B. Banister. Sur. T. B. Banister.
p. B-7

10 July 1787. BARNES, Francis and Elizabeth Mayes, who
writes her own consent. Wit. to consent, Jesse Woodward
and John Jackson. Sur. Jesse Woodward. p. B-4

28 January 1788. BARNES, James and Molly Knight, dau. of
Peter Knight, who consents. Wit. to consent, Isaac Holmes,
Coleman Knight and George Bagley. Sur. Mathew Anderson.
Married by Rev. Charles Anderson. p. B-4

1 April 1812. BARNES, William and Mary Vaden, who writes
her own consent. Wit. to consent, James Chappell and
Mary A. Mann. Sur. James Chappell, who testifies Mary is
of age. p. B-7

27 October 1792. BASKERVILLE, Samuel and Statira Booker.
Sur. Edward Booker. p. B-4

25 August 1791. BASS, Edward and Mary Jones. Sur. William Giles. p. B-4

7 November 1796. BASS, Peter and Elizabeth Mary Ann Jones, dau. of Peter Jones, who consents. Wit. to consent, Edwd Wilkinson and Richd Jones, Junr. Sur. Edward Wilkinson. p. B-5

26 May 1791. BASS, William and Mary Hudson, who writes her own consent. Sur. Wm. C. Hudson. Married by Rev. John Brunskill. p. B-4

16 May 1815. BASS, William C. and Judith J. C. Hudson. Consent of John St. Clair is dated 16 May, 1815. Wit. to consent, Edm^d Scott and William P. Payne. Sur. William P. Payne. p. B-7

14 December 1786. BATES, Abner and Susanna Drinkwater. Sur. James Williams. p. B-3

1 May 1776. BATTE, Richard and Mary Wills, dau. of Lawrence Wills, of Raleigh Parish, who consents and he is surety. p. B-2

24 August 1815. BAUGH, Bartlett and Elizabeth Dyer, who writes her own consent. Wit. to consent, Thomas Purdie, who says each is "upwards of 21." Sur. Thomas Purdie. Married 26 August by Rev. Edmund Goode. p. B-7

24 November 1781. BEASLEY, Robert and Ann Winfree. Sur. Robert Winfree. p. B-2

11 December 1782. BEASLEY, Stephen, Jr. and Rebecca Jones. James Leigh requests this license for "my sister, Rebecca Jones." Wit. to request, A. Elan (?) and Dan'l. Jones. Sur. Peter Beasley. p. B-2

15 November 1806. BEASLEY, William and Patsy McCan, dau. of John Machan, whose consent says, "my daughter, Patsy McCan." Wit. to consent, Robert Ward and Betsey W. Ean (?). Sur. Robert Ward. Married 16 November by Rev. Zachariah G. Leigh, who says Patsy Machan. p. B-5

19 January 1762. BEDEL, John and Rhoda Morris, dau. of Moses Morris, who consents. Wit. to consent, Mary Morris and Tabbitha Morris. Sur. Abraham Bedel. p. B-1

14 August 1782. BELCHER, George and Sally Powell, dau. of George Powell, who consents. Wit. to consent, Daniel Wilkerson and Ann Wilkerson. Sur. Daniel Crawley. p. B-2

23 May 1805. BELCHER, Isaac and Tabitha Webster. Sur. Richard Belcher. p. B-5

24 May 1810. BELCHER, Isaac B. and Lucy Chandler. Sur.
Richard Belcher. Elizabeth Belcher consents. p. B-6

5 July 1779. BELCHER, Jacob and Martha Mann, of this
county. Sur. Frederick Reames. p. B-2

29 March 1804. BELCHER, Joel and Jenny Carpenter, who
writes her own consent. Wit. to consent, Israel (?) Belcher. Sur. Joseph Waldrop. Married 31 March by Rev.
William Dier, who says Jane. p. B-5

2 September 1800. BELCHER, John and Sally Worsham, who
writes her own consent. Sur. Thomas Belcher. p. B-4

3 January 1805. BELCHER, Littleberry and Catherine Roach,
dau. of Jim Roach, who consents. Wit. to consent, John
Belcher who is surety. Married 3 January by Rev. William
Dier. p. B-5

3 January 1787. BELCHER, Richard and Usley Hastin, who
certifies she is of age. Wit. to consent, Sarah Hughes
and Rice Newman. Sur. Sutton Hastin. Married by Rev.
John Brunskill. (Both bond and Minister's Return say
Usley Hastin. K. B. W.) p. B-3

1 December 1810. BELCHER, Robert and Mary Cole, dau. of
Frances Cole, who consents. Wit. to consent, Robt. Tuck.
William Howe testifies each is of age. Sur. William
Stone. p. B-6

25 April 1793. BELCHER, Thomas and Joannah Berry. Sur.
Wm. Archer. p. B-5

22 December 1785. BELCHER, William and Elizabeth Diar.
Sur. Tom Branch Willson. p. B-3

27 May 1790. BELL, Claiborne and Sally Hutchinson, dau.
of Charles Hutcheson, who consents. Wit. to consent, P.
Anderson and Waller Ford. Sur. Paulin Anderson. p. B-4

20 October 1808. BELL, David and Elizabeth Foster, dau.
of Rebecca Foster, who consents. Wit. to consent, George
Bell and Claiborne Bell. Sur. Claiborne Bell. Married
27 October by Rev. John Skurrey. p. B-6

15 March 1813. BELL, George and Nancy Barding. Sur.
William Barding. Wit. to bond, Thomas W. Powell. Married 18 March by Rev. John Skurrey. p. B-7

10 April 1769. BELL, John and Drusilla Hill. Sur. William Ford. p. B-1

13 April 1802. BELL, John and Christiana Roberts. Sur.
Wiley Roberts. John Freeman, Guardian of John Bell, con-
sents and says he is of Nottoway County. Wit. to consent,
Elias Wills and Wiley Roberts. p. B-6

26 November 1799. BELL, Thomas and Sally Robertson, dau.
of James Robertson, who consents. Wit. to consent,
Francis E. Hudson and John Robertson, Jr. Sur. Francis E.
Hudson. p. B-6

27 November 1788. BENNETT, James and Rebecca Harper, dau.
of Wm. Harper, who consents. Wit. to consent, John Smith
and Richard Bennett. This is consent only and not in the
Register.

17 December 1784. BENNETT, Milner and Hester Walton.
Sur. Simeon Walton. p. B-3

30 May 1786. BENNETT, Milner and Mary Bass, dau. of John
Bass, who consents. Wit. to consent, Samuel Bruce and
Elizabeth Bass. Sur. Wm. Keeling. Married by Rev.
Simeon Walton. p. B-3

19 August 1802. BENNETT, Thomas and Frances Johnson.
Sur. Thomas Johnson. Married 3 September by Rev. Charles
Forsee. p. B-6

11 December 1760. BENTLEY, John and Judith Cobbs, spinster. Sur. Thos. Lowry. p. B-1

14 May 1782. BENTLEY, William and Judith Archer. Sur.
John Royall, Jr. p. B-2

8 August 1801. BERRY, Thomas and Lucy Berry. Married by
Rev. John Pollard. Minister's Return.

23 November 1780. BETTS, Spencer and Nancy Fowlkes, dau.
of John Fowlkes, who consents. Sur. Jennings Fowlkes.
p. B-2

22 May 1777. BEUFORD, Henry and Mary Mainyard. Sur.
Thos. G. Peachy, Jr. p. B-2
(The Register has Benford - he signs the bond Beuford.)

13 August 1803. BEVILL, Archer and Polly C. Webster,
who writes her own consent. John Foster testifies she is
"upwards of 21." Sur. John S. Foster. p. B-6

18 June 1797. BEVILL, Claiborne and Ann Talley, who
writes her own consent. Wit. to consent, Richard Walthall and Solomon Coleman. Sur. Martin Chandler. p. B-6

12 March 1785. BEVILL, James and Elizabeth Inge. Sur. Milinton Roach. Wit. to bond, Robert French. p. B-3

14 November 1806. BEVILL, Jarrett and Martha Clay, dau. of Jesse Clay, who consents. Wit. to consent, Robert Clay and Daniel W. Clay. Sur. Robert Clay. p. B-4

28 September 1797. BEVILL, Joel and Sarah Talbot Coleman. Elizabeth Coleman consents. Wit. to consent, John Neal, James Coleman and William Coleman. Sur. James Coleman. p. B-6

12 May 1786. BEVILL, Joseph and Elizabeth Walthall. Sur. Robert Hood. p. B-3

19 October 1803. BEVILL, Robert and Susannah Neal. Sur. Jacob Waddell. p. B-5

20 December 1808. BEVILL, William and Elizabeth Coleman. Sur. Thomas Worsham. p. B-6

6 December 1804. BEVILL, Woodley and Judith W. Brackett, who writes her own consent to Woodley T. Bevill. Consent dated 6 December. Wit. to consent, Ludw. Brackett and Thos. Brackett. Sur. Thos. Brackett Meade. p. B-5 (Register says 5 November - both bond and consent say 6 December. K.B.W.)

12 May 1762. BIBB, William and Hannah Booker. Sur. James Clarke   p. B-1

4 May 1769. BIGGER, John, Jr. and Martha Booker. Sur. Leonard Cheatham, Junr. John is son of John Bigger, Sr., who consents. Wit. to consent, Leonard Cheatham and James Bibb. p. B-1

10 January 1787. BIGGER, Joseph and Elizabeth Macon, who writes her own consent. Wit. to consent, Nancy Bibb and Rebecca W. Macon. Edmund Walker testifies Elizabeth is of age. Sur. Jno: Townes, Jr. p. B-3

19 February 1795. BINNS, Welcher and Sarah Webster, who writes her own consent. Wit. to consent, Peter Webster, Junr. Sur. William Harrison. p. B-6

18 December 1787. BISCOE, Robert and Mary Crenshaw, who writes her own consent. Wit. to consent, Anthony Crenshaw and Thomas Lawton. Sur. Anthony Crenshaw. p. B-3

30 July 1788. BLAKELEY, William, Jr. and Nancy Zachary, who writes her own consent. Wit. to consent, Crawford Zachary and Benjamin Zachary. Sur. William Blakeley. Married by Rev. S. Walton. p. B-4

7 March 1786. BLAND, Edward and Lettice Jones. Sur. Richard Bland. p. B-3

15 September 1814. BLAND, John and Mary B. Perkinson, dau. of Thomas Perkinson, who consents. Wit. to consent, Z. G. Leigh and Abel Jackson. Sur. Zac. G. Leigh. Married 18 September by Rev. Zachariah G. Leigh. p. B-7

26 November 1761. BLAND, Peter and Judith Booker, spinster. Sur. Samuel Terry. p. B-1

29 May 1799. BLANKENSHIP, John and Nancy Mardia. Sur. Micajah Mardia. Married 30 May by Rev. John Skurrey. p. B-6

21 December 1801. BOLES, William and Phebe Boothe, of Amelia, who writes her own consent. Wit. to consent, Jesse Newby. Sur. William Sims. p. B-5

24 December 1782. BOLLING, Alexander and Mary Pryor, dau. of John Pryor, who consents. Sur. Bolling Hall. Wit. to bond, Peter Lamkin, Jr. p. B-2

18 August 1807. BOLLING, Barnett and Jane Williams, who writes her own consent. John Sadler and Lucy Utley testify she is of age. Sur. John Sadler. Married 18 August by Rev. John Skurrey. p. B-4

8 April 1758. BOLLING, Robert and Mary Marshall Tabb. Sur. John Hall. Robert Bolling is of Dinwiddie County. p. B-1

16 December 1779. BOLLING, Robert and Clara Bland. Sur. John T. Peachy. Robert Bolling is of Prince Edward County. p. B-2

16 February 1786. BOLLING, Thos. Tabb and Seigniora Peyton. Sur. Isaac Holmes. p. B-3

23 January 1799. BOOKER, Daniel and Mary Winston. Sur. James Henderson. p. B-5

1 September 1800. BOOKER, Davis and Sarah Booker. Sur. John C. Cobbs. Married 2 September by Rev. John Skurrey. p. B-4

17 ---- 1746. BOOKER, Edmund, Jr. and Edith M. Cobbs, dau. of Samuel Cobbs. Sur. John Nash. p. B-1

28 June 1781. BOOKER, Edmond and Mary Pride. Sur. James Hill. Wit. to bond, Milton Roach. p. B-2

21 February 1739. BOOKER, Edward, Jr. and Ann Cobbs, dau. of Sam'l Cobbs. Sur. Samuel Tarry. p. B-1

30 September 1761. BOOKER, Edward and Mary Bentley. Sur. Samuel Bentley. p. B-1

18 August 1783. BOOKER, Edmund, Jr. and Mary Harwood Clements, dau. of Isham Clements, who consents. Sur. Thos. Whitworth. p. B-2

27 October 1783. BOOKER, Edward and Fdith Cobbs Anderson. Sur. Edmund Walker. p. B-2

25 February 1783. BOOKER, Efford and Mary Hudson. Sur. R. Booker. p. B-2
(In the top of the bond is Richard Booker - he signs, R.)

12 October 1745. BOOKER, George and Sarah Cobbs. Sur. Richard Booker. Wit. to bond, Samuel Cobbs. p. B-1

24 June 1746. BOOKER, John and Phebe Worsham. Sur. Will Booker. Judith Booker's consent is dated 5 ____ 1746. Wit. to consent, Edward Booker and Wm. Maycock. Gov. William Gooch also consents. p. B-1

4 December 1764. BOOKER, John and Susanna Pride, dau. of John Pride, who consents. Sur. Francis Anderson. p. B-1

15 May 1800. BOOKER, Parham and Elizabeth L. Overton, dau. of Mary Overton, who consents. Wit. to consent, Waller Ford and John Hurt. Sur. Waller Ford. Married 29 May by Rev. John Skurrey. p. B-5

22 February 1787. BOOKER, Pinkethman Davis and Martha Pride, who writes her own consent. Wit. to consent, John Collie and George Booker. Sur. George Booker. p. B-3

21 June 1763. BOOKER, Richard and Martha Robertson. Sur. Thos. Gray. p. B-1

27 December 1784. BOOKER, Richard and Jane Hudson. Sur. Davis Booker. p. B-3

16 September 1796. Booker, Richard and Sarah Cobbs. Sur. Thos. Turpin. p. B-5

14 December 1815. BOOKER, Richerson and Ann D. Booker, who writes her own consent. Wit. to consent, P. L. Townes and Sally B. Rison. Sur. P. L. Townes. Married 17 December by Rev. John Skurrey, who says Richeson Booker. p. B-7

23 December 1784. BOOKER, Samuel and Martha Munford, dau. of James Munford. Sur. James Townes, Jr. p. B-2

4 February 1785. BOOKER, Samuel and Rachel Jones. Sur. John Booker. p. B-3

1 April 1755. BOOKER, William and Mary Flournoy. Sur. Edmund Booker, Jr. pp. B-1, B-2

14 May 1768. BOOKER, William, Jr. and Edith Booker, dau. of George Booker of Raleigh Parish, whose consent is dated 7 May 1768. Sur. Sam'l Cobbs. Thomas Tabb gives consent for this marriage. Wit. to his consent, Sam'l Cobbs and Sally Booker. p. B-1

17 December 1812. BOOKER, William M. and Sally L. (?) Blankenship, dau. of John Blankenship, who consents. Wit. to consent, John F. Jackson, Sam'l Blankenship and Sally S. Blankenship. Sur. John F. Blankenship. Married by Rev. Zachariah G. Leigh. p. B-7

25 February 1784. BOOTH, Charles and Ann Stratton. Sur. Charles Old. p. B-3

9 October 1795. BOOTH, John and Ann Ford, who writes her own consent. Wit. to consent, Sam'l Ford and Martha Ford. Sam'l Ford testifies Ann is of age. Sur. John Chappell. p. B-4

18 January 1768. BOOTH, William and Elizabeth Johns, dau. of John Johns of Nottoway Parish, who consents. Wit. to consent, John Howson and John Johns. Sur. John Howson. p. B-1

25 September 1788. BORUM, Benjamin and Sally Thompson, dau. of Mary Thompson, who consents. Wit. to consent, John Elsen (?) and _____ Richardson. Sur. Jesse Green. p. B-4

17 October 1765. BORUM, Edmund and Edith Seay, dau. of Jacob Seay of Raleigh Parish, who consents. Wit. to consent, Robert Powell and Phebe Seay. Sur. John Booker. p. B-1

12 December 1808. BORUM, James and Elizabeth Harper. Her Guardian, Thompson Scott, requests this license. Wit. to request, James Harper and Nancy Waddill. Sur. James Harper. Married 22 December by Rev. Thomas Pettus. p. B-5

17 January 1753. BOSWELL, Joseph and Elizabeth Elliott, dau. of George Elliott, who is surety. Joseph Boswell is a millwright of Amelia County. p. B-1

24 November 1757. BOTT, Miles and Sarah Neal, spinster.
Sur. Jeremiah Kean. p. B-1

24 October 1780. BOTTOM, Miles and Clary Callicott, dau.
of James and Clary Callicott, who consent. (Callicoat?)
Sur. John Bottom. Miles is son of Thomas Bottom, who
consents. p. B-2

29 September 1788. BOURDON, Nicholas and Martha Dennis.
Sur. John Royall, who, as Martha's guardian, requests
this license. p. B-4

24 August 1809. BOWLES, Hezekiah and Betsey Robertson,
who writes her own consent. Wit. to consent, James Henderson, who is surety. p. B-5

3 January 1791. BOWMAN, William and Betsy Jolley. Sur.
William Hanson. p. B-4

27 April 1758. BOWRY, Mr. and Elizabeth Morgan, dau. of
James Morgan, who consents. Wit. to consent, Jno. James
and Wm. Jones. This is consent only - not in the Register.

28 January 1808. BOWRY, William and Elizabeth B. Drake,
dau. of William Drake, who consents. Wit. to consent,
Thos. Worsham, A. Coleman and Jesse Southall. Sur.
Thomas Worsham. p. B-5

26 December 1792. BOYD, Francis and Alice Worsham, who
writes her own consent. Wit. to consent, Archer Worsham
and Francis Boyd, Jr. Sur. Archer Worsham. Married by
Rev. John Brunskill. p. B-5
(Others have copied her name as ANN; the bond has Alice
and she signs her consent Alice.)

17 June 1783. BRACKETT, Ludwell and Ann Cox. Sur. Henry
Cox. p. B-2

4 December 1781. BRADBURY, William and Susanna Webster.
Sur. Simon Morgan. p. B-2

9 November 1805. BRADLEY, George M. (?) and Sarah Walden.
Caleb Green consents and says Sarah is daughter of John
Walden. Wit. to consent, John Walden and William Walden.
Married 9 November by Rev. John Skurrey. p. B-6

7 August 1811. BRADLEY, Joseph and Rebecca Booth, who
writes her consent. Wit. to her consent, Matt. Booth.
She is dau. of Elizabeth Booth, who also consents. Wit.
to Elizabeth's consent, Matt. Booth and Jesse Booth.
Sur. Jesse Southall. p. B-7

7 December 1784. BRADSHAW, Jeremiah and Dicey Jeter, who writes her own consent. Sur. William Jones. p. B-3

11 October 1787. BRADSHAW, John, Junr. and Winny Brooks, who writes her own consent. Wit. to consent, James Bevill and John Holt. Sur. John Holt. p. B-3

23 October 1788. BRADSHAW, Thomas and Polly Borum. Edmund Borum consents. Wit. to consent, Robert Anderson, George Bagley and Joseph Hubbard. Sur. Benjamin Borum. p. B-4

26 December 1783. BRADSHAW, William and Mary Kirkland. Sur. James Stott. p. B-2

23 June 1801. BRADSHAW, William and Tempey Foster. Sur. James Stott. p. B-6

6 April 1808. BRAGG, Joseph and Ann Willson. Sur. Daniel Willson. p. B-4

11 December 1807. BRAGG, Thomas N. and Elizabeth Murray, dau. of Nancy Murray, who consents and says Thomas is of Chesterfield County. Wit. to consent, John Rogers and Henry B. Jones. Sur. John Rogers. p. B-5

9 February 1793. BRAME, John and Frances Coleman, dau. of Daniel Coleman, Senr., who consents. Wit. to consent, Daniel Coleman, Jr., Martha Coleman and Fatha Coleman. Sur. Daniel Coleman. Married 14 February by Rev. Robert Walthall, who says John Brame, Planter. p. B-5

5 January 1801. BRANCH, Benjamin and Sarah Bott, dau. of Miles Bott, whose consent is dated 5 January. Wit. to consent, Nathan Bott. Sur. William Bott. p. B-6

6 July 1764. BRANCH, Edward and Lucy Finney, who writes her own consent. Sur. Branch Tanner. p. B-1

5 November 1787. BRANCH, Edward and Martha Bott, dau. of Miles Bott, who consents. Wit. to consent, John Thacher. Sur. John Archer. Married by Rev. John Brunskill. p. B-3

-- February 1749. BRANCH, Matt--- and (obliterated) (Ridley Jones (?)). Sur. Peter Jones. p. B-1

24 March 1785. BRANCH, Peter and Judith Jones, dau. of John Jones. Sur. Thomas Miller. p. B-3

26 December 1789. BRANCH, Thomas and Nancy Clements, dau. of Isham Clements, who consents. Wit. to consent, John Phillips and Frances E. Harris. Sur. Wm. Clements. Married 31 December by Rev. Jesse Talley. p. B-4

19 December 1792. BRANCH, Thomas and Mary Walker, dau. of Edmund Walker, who consents. Sur. Samuel Flournoy. p. B-4

20 September 1764. BRANCH, William and Judith Scott. Sur. John Scott. p. B-1

28 October 1791. BRANCH, William and Dicey Callicott. James Callicott and John Archer request this license. Married by Rev. John Brunskill. Returned 30 December, 1791. (This marriage is not in the Register.)

26 November 1812. BRANCH, William, Jr. and Jane Davis Booker. Her Guardian, Moses Coleman, consents on 24 November and says she is orphan of Col. Edmund Booker, and William Branch, Jr. is of Prince Edward County. Wit. to consent, Curtis B. Atwood.and Richard Phillips, Jr. Sur. Carter B. Atkins. Married 26 November by Rev. John Pollard. p. B-7

21 December 1785. BRAY, William and Sally Hensly, dau. of Lucy Hensly, who consents. Wit. to consent, Arthur Leath and Molley Leath. Sur. Charles Lovesay. Married 23 December by Rev. Devereux Jarratt. p. B-3

16 April 1794. BREWER, John and Usley Kidd, dau. of George Kidd, whose consent says, my daughter, Uslee Kidd. Wit. to consent, Stephen South and George Kidd. Sur. George Kidd. p. B-5

30 March 1809. BRIZENDINE, Joshua and Elizabeth Farris, who writes her consent to Joshua Britain Brizendine. Wit. to consent, W. W. Hall. Sur. Wm. W. Hall. p. B-6

1 August 1795. BROADDUS, Richard and Mine Jeter, who writes her own consent. Wit. to consent, Peter Dupuy, Jr. and Wm. Broaddus. Sur. William Broaddus. p. B-5

25 August 1796. BROADFOOT, Charles and Purify B. Willson. Sur. John Finney. p. B-6

11 December 1801. BROADNAX, Edward B. and Frances Brooking, dau. of V. Brooking, whose consent says, Frances V. Brooking. Wit. to consent, Edwd B. Brooking and Francis Brooking. Sur. Francis Brooking. p. B-5

22 January 1793. BROADNAX, William and Ann Brooking, dau. of V. Brooking, who consents. Wit. to consent, Wm. Brooking and Henry T. Brooking. Sur. Henry T. Brooking. p. B-6

28 June 1787. BROADWAY, John and Sarah Pollard. Sur. Peter Clarke. p. B-4

24 March 1785. BROOKS, John and Sarah Neal. Sur. Abraham Hatchett. p. B-3

25 October 1787. BROOKS, Moses and Elizabeth Furguson. Sur. Susanna Furguson. Married by Rev. Charles Anderson. p. B-4

15 September 1807. BROUGHTON, John and Elizabeth Tucker. Absalom Tucker requests this license. Wit. to request, Francis Tucker and William Tucker. Sur. Daniel Orvill. p. B-5

2 January 1813. BROWDER, David and Mary Coleman. John Southall, her Guardian, consents and says Sarah Marye Coleman. Wit. to consent, Jesse Coleman and Henry H. Southall. Sur. Jesse Coleman. Married 7 January by Rev. James Chappell. p. B-7

7 July 1813. BROWDER, George and Martha Hawks, who writes her own consent. Wit. to consent, David Mann and Martha Mann. David Hawks testifies she is of age. Sur. David Mann. p. B-7

17 June 1799. BROWN, Bennett and Mary C. Royall, who writes her own consent. Wit. to consent, Ann Hill and Martha Roberts. Sur. Parham Booker. Married 18 June by Rev. John Skurrey. p. B-5

24 June 1813. BROWN, Herbert and Betsy Bevill. Sur. Pleasant Bevill. p. B-7

27 November 1795. BROWN, Joseph and Ann Worsham, dau. of Thomas Worsham, who consents and says Joseph Brown is of Nottoway County. Wit. to consent, William Worsham and Francis Gooch. Sur. Francis Gooch. p. B-5

5 February 1799. BROWN, Joseph and Salley Robertson. Nathan Robertson, Salley's Guardian, consents. Wit. to consent, John Robertson and John Mitchell. Sur. John Robertson. Married 14 February by Rev. John Skurrey. p. B-4

24 April 1783. BRUCE, Alexr and Martha Johns. Sur. John Harrison. p. B-2

11 December 1788. BRUCE, Armistead and Elizabeth Bass, dau. of John Bass, who consents. Wit. to consent, Jno. Bass, Jr. and Isaac Holmes. This is consent only and not in the Register.

26 October 1786. BRUCE, Samuel and Agnes Bass. Sur. John Bass. Married by Rev. Simeon Walton. p. B-3

27 November 1792. BRUMFIELD, William and Polly Butler.
Sur. William Butler. p. B-6

28 January 1792. BRYAN, Banister and Judith Clements,
dau. of Isham Clements, who consents. Wit. to consent,
William Clements, who is surety. p. B-4

25 August 1785. BRYAN, William and Ann Hundley, dau. of
Ann Hundley, who consents. Wit. to consent, John Thornton. Sur. William Hundley. Married by Rev. Simeon Walton. p. B-3

7 February 1806. BURFOOT, Thomas and Mary E. Cousins,
dau. of Elizabeth Cousins, who consents. (Her consent
says Thomas Burfoot and he so signs the bond.) Wit. to
consent, John C. Cousins and Robert Cousins. Sur.
Robert Cousins. p. B-6

29 April 1811. BURFOOT, Thomas, Sr. and Rebecca Mann.
Field Mann, who requests this license, says Thomas Burfoot is of Chesterfield County. Sur. Ben. W. Leigh.
p. B-6

28 November 1784. BURGE, William and Martha Williamson,
dau. of Lewelling Williamson, who consents. Consent
dated 27 November 1784. Sur. Raines Cooke. p. B-3

4 September 1778. BURKS, Charles and Rebeckah Baldwin,
dau. of William Baldwin, whose consent says she is under age. Sur. John Baldwin. p. B-2

27 December 1787. BURKS, Philemon and Edith Jackson.
Sur. Arthur Jackson. p. B-3

26 January 1749. BURKS, Richard and Milliner Hawkins.
Sur. Benj^a Hawkins. p. B-1

9 September 1782. BURT, Robert and Ritta Anderson. Sur.
John Anderson. p. B-2

28 March 1793. BURTON, Abraham and Prudence Webster,
dau. of John Webster, who consents. Wit. to consent,
William Burton and William Trige(?). Sur. Dennis
Minge. (Others have copied this, Abraham Benton -
Burton is in top of bond, he signs Burton, and Burton
is in the consent.) p. B-5

23 July 1795. BURTON, Allen and Sally Goodwyn. Her
affidavit she is 21 years of age. Sur. James Craddock. p. B-5

3 December 1781. BURTON, John and Martha Cocke Farley,
of Raleigh Parish. Sur. William Craddock. p. B-2

22 December 1800. BURTON, Samuel and Susannah Morris, dau. of Moses Morris, who consents. Wit. to consent, William Morris and James Ellis. Sur. James Ellis. Married by Rev. David Thomson. p. B-6

14 May 1782. BURTON, Thomas and Martha Seay, of this county. Sur. Samuel Burton. p. B-2

9 April 1782. BURTON, William and Mary Ann Ellis, of this county. Sur. Samuel Burton. p. B-2

-- ---- 1787. BURTON, William and Lucy Hazlegrove. Sur. Archer Coleman. On August 27, ---- Sebet Bevill consents for William Burton to get a marriage license. There is no year given in the consent, but it is with those for 1787. Wit. to consent, Burrel Coleman and James Bevill. p. B-3

16 November 1788. BURTON, William and Oney Morris, dau. of Moses Morris, who consents. Wit. to consent, Andrew Christian and William Burton. Sur. Walter Morris. p. B-4

-- ----- ----. BURTON, William and Branch Morris. Married by Rev. John Pollard. This marriage is in a list dated: "Since October 1788". Minister's Return.

20 July 1807. BURTON, William and Nancy Meador, who writes her own consent. She is daughter of Elizabeth Meador, who requests this license. Wit. to consent and to request, Thomas Meador and Abraham Meador. Sur. Abraham Meador. p. B-5

10 October 1803. BURWELL, Lewis and Sally E. Green, dau. of Abraham Green, whose consent says, Sary E. Green. Wit. to consent, Will^th Waugh and John Broughton. Sur. John Townes. p. B-6

12 October 1797. BUSBY, Robert and Nancy Foster, dau. of Edith Foster, who consents. Wit. to consent, George Baldwin and Wm. A. Baldwin. Sur. George Baldwin. p. B-6

13 January 1789. BUTLER, Archibald and Milly Clardy, dau. of Benjamin Clardy, who consents. Wit. to consent, John Gifford and William Clardy. Sur. Thomas Morriss. p. B-4

12 October 1791. BUTLER, Isaac and Rebecckah Noble, dau. of Joseph Noble, who consents for his daughter, Rebekah. Wit. to consent, Zachariah Butler. Sur. Josiah Noble. p. B-4

25 September 1788. BUTLER, John and Sarah Clardy. Sur. John Crawley. p. B-4

9 July 1782. BUTLER, William and Martha Farley. Peter
Ellington consents for Martha. Wit. to consent, "Thomas
(Seal)" and "William (Seal)". Sur. Sterling Williams.
p. B-2

16 February 1799. BUTLER, William and Patsy Rucker, dau.
of Samuel Rucker, who consents. Wit. to consent, Zachariah Butler, who is surety. p. B-6

6 December 1787. BUTLER, Zachariah and Elizabeth Noble,
dau. of Joseph Noble, who consents. Wit. to consent,
Thomas Osborne and William Pillow. Sur. William Butler.
Married by Rev. John Pollard. p. B-3

13 April 1779. CABINESS, George and Sarah Jennings. A
note from Samuel Thompson and Jos. Jennings, 12 April,
1779, requests this license and says, "Sarah is of that
age and Capable to act for herself with Respect to marriage." Sur. Robert French. p. C-2

24 December 1781. CABINESS, Henry and Jane Williams.
Married by Rev. Jeremiah Walker. Returned 2 May 1782.
Minister's Return.

16 March 1784. CAFFERY, Barnard and Agnes Jennings, dau.
of William Jennings, Jr., whose consent says **Bernard**
Caffery. Sur. Woodward Jennings. p. C-2

24 June 1790. CANNON, William and Elizabeth Cocke,
who writes her own consent. Wit. to consent, John Archer
and Stephen Cook. Sur. John Archer. p. C-3

6 November 1809. CARDWELL, Francis and Martha C. Westbrook. Sur. Joshua Hawks, Jr. p. C-4

27 August 1785. CARDWELL, Perin and Betsey Worsham,
dau. of Henry Worsham, whose consent says **Perry** Cardwell. Sur. William Fleming. p. C-2

11 September 1787. CARDWELL, Thomas and Mary A. Freeman,
dau. of William Freeman, who consents. Wit. to consent,
Anderson Freeman and Evans Freeman. Sur. Evans Freeman.
Married by Rev. John Brunskill. p. C-3

10 July 1782. CARLEY, John and Elizabeth MacKintire.
Married by Rev. Charles Anderson. Minister's Return.

27 November 1800. CARPENTER, Benjamin and Nancy Claiborne.
Sur. Leonard Claiborne. p. C-4

8 December 1802. CARPENTER, Benjamin and Usle Braxenian
(?). Sur. Bartholomew Kidd. p. C-4

6 January 1797. CARPENTER, Samuel and Jean Hundley, dau.
of Elizabeth Hundley. Sur. John McLaurine. p. C-4

27 September 1790. CARR, Hezekiah and Edith Parsons Raglin. Sur. Joseph Raglin. Married by Rev. Robert Walthall
who says Hezekiah Carr, waggoner. p. C-3

5 February 1806. CARTER, Coleman and Mary Wingo. Sur.
William Holt. Married 5 February by Rev. John Pollard.
p. C-5

13 September 1815. CARTER, Thomas and Catharine Muse,
who writes her own consent. Wit. to consent, John W.
Foster and James W. Muse. Sur. John W. Foster. p. C-5

14 October 1784. CASHON, James and Nancy Weeks. Sur.
William Green. p. C-2

10 March 1785. CAUDLE, Richard and Elizabeth Locke. who
writes her own consent. Sur. Abner Bates. Wit. to bond,
Robert French. p. C-2

4 January 1809. CHAFFIN, John and Eliza Booker. Sur.
William Booker. Wit. to bond, John Lane. p. C-3

11 October 1800. CHAFFIN, Joshua and Patty Giles. Sur.
James Townes, Jr. Married 13 October by Rev. David
Thomson. p. C-3

11 December 1783. CHANDLER, Claiborne and Elizabeth
Dobson. Married by Rev. Charles Anderson. Minister's
Return.

13 August 1812. CHANDLER, Spencer and Keziah Belcher,
who writes her own consent. Sur. Newby Belcher. Martin
Chandler gives consent for Spencer. Wit. to each consent, William Chandler and Newby Belcher. p. C-5

12 November 1807. CHANDLER, William and Judith Belcher.
Sur. Parham Reese. p. C-4

27 January 1791. CHAPMAN, John and Amey Seay, who
writes her own consent. Sur. William Pollard. p. C-3

18 December 1799. CHAPMAN, John and Oney League, dau.
of James League. Sur. Christopher Hubbard. Married
21 December by Rev. John Skurrey. p. C-5

21 December 1792. CHAPMAN, William and Ann Jones. Sur.
Moses Pollard. Married 23 December by Rev. John Skurrey.
p. C-5

4 September 1786. CHAPPELL, Abner and Susanna Moore. John Tucker, her Guardian, consents. Sur. John Tucker. p. C-3

17 November 1767. CHAPPELL, James and Phebe Archer, of Raleigh Parish, who writes her own consent. Her consent is dated 16 November, 1767. Sur. John Archer. p. C-1

12 February 1806. CHAPPELL, James and Nancy F. Vaden, dau. of Henry Vaden. Sur. David Mann. p. C-4

28 June 1765. CHAPPELL, John and Sarah Hurt, spinster, dau. of Moses and Ann Hurt, who consent. Wit. to consent, Moses Hurt and Joseph White. Sur. John Hightower. John Chappell is of Nottoway Parish. p. C-1

23 October 1788. CHAPPELL, John and Dorothy Ford, dau. of Lucy Ford, whose consent says Dorothea. Wit. to consent, Sam[l] Ford and Milton Ford. Sur. William Ford. p. C-3

2 April 1800. CHAPPELL, John and Elizabeth T. Craddock. Charles Craddock's consent says Elizabeth Townes Craddock. Wit. to consent, Edmund Morton and Milton Vaughan. Sur. Edward Maston. Married 10 or 16 April (two lists) by Rev. John Skurrey. p. C-4

24 April 1783. CHAPPELL, Miles and Sarah Mann. Sur. Cain Mann. p. C-2

21 November 1759. CHAPPELL, Robert and Agnes Cross. Consent of William Cross says Robert Chappell is of Dinwiddie County. Wit. to consent, Elizabeth Cross and Betty May. Sur. Daniel Jones. p. C-1

4 March 1791. CHAPPELL, Robert and Peggy Williamson, dau. of Lewelling Williamson. who consents. Sur. Joseph Rogers. Married by Rev. John Brunskill. p. C-3

25 May 1786. CHAPPELL, Samuel and Martha Perkinson. Sur. Rice Newman. p. C-3

17 November 1747. CHEATHAM, Benj. and Grace Williams. Sur. Thomas Brooks. Benj. Cheatham is of Henrico County. p. C-1

14 November 1785. CHEATHAM, Joel and Rhoda League. Sur. William Barding. p. C-2

4 March 1786. CHEATHAM, Joel and Elizabeth Hundley, dau. of Ann Hundley, who consents. Wit. to consent, Joshua Hundley and William Bryan. Sur. Joshua Hundley. Married by Rev. Charles Anderson. Listed twice, pp. C-2 and C-3

17 April 1769. CHEATHAM, Leonard and Mary Booker, of Raleigh Parish. Sur. William Booker. p. C-1

11 November 1809. CHIEVES, John and Anney Jones. Sur. Jesse Leath. p. C-4

31 October 1810. CHIEVES, Peter L. and Polly Marshall. Sur. John Chieves, who testifies Polly is of age. p. C-5

20 ---- ----. CHILDRA, Wm. and Keturah Haskins. Sur. Benj. Haskins. p. C-1

20 December 1780. CHILDRESS, John and Sarah Booker. Sur. Millington Roach. Wit. to bond, Richard Jones, Jr. and _____ Fitzgerald. p. C-2

18 November 1782. CHILDRESS, William and Frankey Rice. Nich[l] Watters consents for "Miss Frankey Rice." Sur. Robert Childress. p. C-2

28 November 1790. CHRISTIAN, Andrew and Polly Hatton. Sur. Thomas Hatton. p. C-3

7 November 1755. CHRISTIAN, Anthony and Mary Watkins, widow. Sur. Andrew Wade. p. C-1

13 April 1783. CHUMLEY, John and Elizabeth Dicken. Sur. Jacob Utley. Benjamin Locket certifies that Martha Chumley consents for her son, John. p. C-2

28 January 1802. CLAIBORNE, James and Sarah Brooking, dau. of Vivion Brooking. Sur. Francis Brooking. p. C-4

28 November 1794. CLAIBORNE, John and Martha Reames. Sur. Wm. Wilkinson. p. C-5

22 September 1796. CLAIBORNE, John and Hetty (Katy?) Hamblin. "Her own certificate says Hetty." Sur. Peter Jones. p. C-3

24 November 1803. CLAIBORNE, John and Elizabeth Cousins, dau. of William Cousins. Sur. Robert Coleman. p. C-3

13 November 1788. CLAIBORNE, Leonard and Fanny Tanner. Sur. Robert Tanner. p. C-3

17 April 1755. CLAIBORNE, Richard and Mary Hamlin, spinster, dau. of Charles Hamlin, who consents. Wit. to consent, Thomas Claiborne and Charles Hamlin, Jr. Sur. Thomas Claiborne. Wit. to bond, Sam[l] Cobbs and William Callicoat. Richard Claiborne, carpenter. p. C-1

28 January 1768. CLAIBORNE, William and Mary Williamson, dau. of Joseph Williamson, who consents. Wit. to consent, Will Watts and George Hightower. Sur. William Wat---. p. C-1

14 August 1802. CLARDY, Archer and Martha Nunnally, who writes her consent, dated 14 August 1802, and says, "I am my own woman and has been for nine years." Wit. to consent, Richard Powell. Sur. Joel Harris. (Both bond and consent are dated 14 August.) p. C-4

15 July 1766. CLARK, John and Ann Hudson, who writes her own consent. Wit. to consent, William Hudson and Betty Hudson. Sur. William Hudson. p. C-1

10 March 1787. CLARKE, John and Hannah Cabiness, dau. of Mathew Cabiness, whose consent says Hannah is of age. Wit. to consent, _____ C. Clarke. Sur. William Clarke. Married by Rev. Charles Anderson. p. C-3

27 March 1799. CLARKE, Lewis and Mary Ligon Moseley. George Rowlett testifies she is of age. Sur. Thomas B. Moseley. p. C-4

16 February 1786. CLARKE, Peter and Ann Bonner, who writes her own consent. Wit. to consent, Jno. Royall and Sam¹ Pryor. Sur. William Clarke. Married 18 February by Rev. Devereux Jarratt. p. C-2

10 April 1736. CLARKE, Richard and Lucy Booker. Sur. James Clarke. (See D. B. L, p. 539) p. C-1

5 December 1797. CLARKE, Turner and Lucy Holt. Sur. Richard Holt. Married 9 December by Rev. John Skurrey. p. C-4

5 December 1786. CLARKE, William and Ann Beasley, dau. of Anne Beasley, whose consent says Ann is dau. of John Beasley. Wit. to consent, Richd Ligon. Sur. John Hall. Married by Rev. Simeon Walton. p. C-3

18 October 1786. CLAY, Charles and Mary Hawks. Sur. Richard Hawks. p. C-3

6 June 1804. CLAY, Charles and Amy Epes. Sur. Thos. Booth. Married 9 June by Rev. John Jones, Methodist. p. C-5

26 September 1814. CLAY, Charles and Martha Dyer, who writes her own consent. Wit. to consent, Peter Burton and Daniel Dier. Sur. Peter Burton. Married 3 October by Rev. James Chappell. p. C-5

19 December 1815. CLAY, Daniel and Nancy B. Waugh, dau. of Andrew Waugh. Sur. Anderson Tucker. p. C-5

30 March 1792. CLAY, David and Martha Clay. Sur. Dancy Adams. p. C-4

9 February 1790. CLAY, Jesse and Hannah Coleman. Sur. Daniel Coleman. p. C-3

17 November 1783. CLAY, John and Fanny Allen, dau. of Daniel Allen, of this County, who is surety. p. C-2

18 September 1809. CLAY, John and Dolly Coleman. William and Anderson Coleman testify Dolly is of age. Sur. William Coleman. p. C-4

14 October 1769. CLAY, John, Jr. and Sarah Chappell, dau. of James Chappell. Sur. John Clay. p. C-2

10 May 1756. CLAY, William and Ann Old, dau. of John Old, who consents. Wit. to consent, John Clay and Charles Clay. Sur. John Clay. p. C-1

18 April 1803. CLAYBROOK, Samuel and Nancy Barding, who writes her own consent. Sur. William Barding. Married 21 April by Rev. John Pollard, who says Mary. p. C-3

26 January 1792. CLAYBROOK, William and Amelia Whitlock. Sur. Peter Claybrook. Married 29 January by Rev. Abner Watkins. p. C-3

27 December 1781. CLEMENT, Edward and Elizabeth Harriss. Sur. John James. p. C-2

27 November 1760. CLEMENT, Isham and Sarah Scott, spinster. Sur. Alexr Walker. p. C-1

2 December 1745. CLEMENT, John and Frances Booker. Sur. Edmd Booker. p. C-1

7 September 1789. CLEMENTS, John and Nancy Walthall, dau. of William Walthall, who consents. Wit. to consent, Henry Walthall and Stephen Beasley. Sur. John Clay. John Clemons consents for John Clements. p. C-3

19 December 1796. CLEMENTS, Joseph and Susannah A. Woodson, dau. of Joseph Woodson. Sur. John Chaffin. p. C-4

17 December 1764. CLEMENTS, William and Ann Clay, spinster. Sur. William Puryear. p. C-1

25 December 1799. CLEMENT, William and Polly Clarke Craddock, dau. of Charles Craddock. Sur. George Owen. Married 26 December by Rev. John Skurrey. p. C-4

23 November 1758. CLEMENT, William, Jr. and Ann Walker,
spinster. Sur. Edwd Walker. p. C-1

14 April 1767. COBBS, John Catlin and Rachel Smith.
Sur. Richard Booker. (See D. B. 9, p. 247 - bond is
mutilated.) p. C-1

8 December 1768. COBBS, Samuel and Elizabeth Munford.
Sur. John C. Cobbs. p. C-1

16 January 1812. COBBS, Thomas M. and Nancy I. Hurt, dau.
of Anson Hurt, who is surety. p. C-5

11 April 1769. COCKE, Chastain and Martha Field Archer,
dau. of William Archer of Raleigh Parish, who consents.
Wit. to consent, John Archer. Sur. Peter Farrar. p. C-1

4 June 1794. COCKE, James and Mary Lewis, dau. of Eliz.
Lewis. Sur. John Royall. p. C-4

24 November 1767. COCKE, James Powell and Elizabeth
Archer. William Archer consents. Wit. to consent, John
Archer and Charles Lewis. Sur. Henry Anderson. p. C-1

4 December 1764. COCKE, Stephen and Amey Jones, dau. of
Richard Jones, who consents. Wit. to consent, Lewelling
Jones and Andrew Redford. Sur. Lewelling Jones. p. C-1

23 February 1779. COCKE, Thomas and Margaret Jones, of
Nottoway Parish. Sur. Stith Hardaway. p. C-2

18 July 1787. COFFEE, Thomas and Mary Knight, dau. of
Charles Knight, who consents. Wit. to consent, Matthew
Anderson and Coleman Knight. Sur. Coleman Knight. Mar-
ried by Rev. Charles Anderson. p. C-3

28 September 1769. COGBILL, Charles and Frances Bottom.
Sur. Thomas Bottom. p. C-1

29 December 1787. COLEMAN, Archer and Liza Bevill, dau.
of James Bevill, who consents. Wit. to consent, Burwell
Coleman and Robert Bevill. Sur. John Southall. Married
by Rev. John Brunskill. p. C-3

22 July 1782. COLEMAN, Burrel (Burwell?) and Lucy Bevill,
dau. of James Bevill, who consents. Wit. to consent,
James Clardy and James Bevill. Sur. James Clardy. p. C-2

13 March 1782. COLEMAN, Cain and Mary Wilson. Sur. John
Wilson. Cain is son of Daniel Coleman, who consents.
p. C-2

30 December 1805. COLEMAN, Jesse and Frances Southall,
dau. of John Southall. Sur. "Burned" Southall. p. C-5

26 March 1807. COLEMAN, John and Mary Talley, dau. of
John Talley. Sur. Wm. H. Cabell. p. C-4

4 May 1799. COLEMAN, Robert and Elizabeth Perkinson.
Sur. Joel Perkinson. p. C-4

24 February 1787. COLEMAN, Solomon and Mildred Perkinson,
dau. of Jeremiah Perkinson, who consents. Wit. to consent,
Robert Bevill, Sam Purkinson and Mildred Perkinson. Sur.
Isaac Coleman. p. C-3

1 October 1796. COLEMAN, William and Nancy Clay, dau. of
Jesse Clay. Sur. Henry N. Southall. p. C-5

6 December 1809. COLLEY, James and Polly Ferguson, dau.
of Robert Ferguson, who consents. Wit. to consent,
George Brown and James Worsham. Sur. James Worsham.
Married 8 December by Rev. John Pollard, Senr. p. C-5

9 March 1807. COLLEY, Matthew and Ann Rison. Sur. Ellery
Rison. Wit. to bond, Bentley Anderson. p. C-4

11 September 1750. COMBS, John and Frances Elam. Sur.
John Booker. Wit. to bond, Samuel Cobbs and Wm. May
Cock(?) p. C-1

23 May 1783. COMER, Thomas and Elizabeth Robertson.
Sur. Peter Lumkin. p. C-2
(23 May is inside the bond, 22 May on outside the bond.)

18 December 1784. COMPTON, Archibald and Sally Cavender,
dau. of Hugh Cavender, who consents. Wit. to consent,
Ambrose Jeter. Sur. Jeremiah Compton. p. C-2

25 October 1784. COMPTON, Jeremiah and Betsy Cavender,
dau. of Hugh Cavender, who consents. Wit. to consent,
Francis Cavender and Betsey Cavender. Sur. Joseph
Cavender. p. C-2

14 December 1786. COMPTON, Joel and Nancy Chapman, dau.
of John Chapman, Sr., who consents. Wit. to consent, John
Chapman, junr. and Benj. Chapman. Sur. Benjamin Chapman.
p. C-3

23 December 1783. COMPTON, Vincent and Frances Williams, who writes her own consent. Wit. to consent, Philip Williams, junr. and Joel Mottley. Sur. Thos. Self. p. C-2

14 March 1789. CONNALLY, Jno. William and Peggy Sallard, dau. of Charles Sallard, who consents. Wit. to consent, Charles Sallard, Jr. and Rebecca Sallard. Sur. W. P. Jackson. p. C-3 This consent is dated 13 March, 1789.

14 July 1796. CONWAY, Archer and Polly French. Sur. Robert Dickey. p. C-4

27 September 1764. COOK, James and Anna Ford. Sur. Jno. Mc_____. p. C-2

20 November 1784. COOK, Raines and Elizabeth Williamson. William Cross Craddock consents and says Elizabeth is of age and consents. Sur. William Burge. p. C-2

23 December 1784. COOK, Thomas and Martha Vaughan, dau. of Robert Vaughan, who consents. Wit. to consent, Joel Mottley, James Cook and Philip Williams, junr. This is consent only.

7 August 1810. COOPER, James and Jane Haskins, who writes her own consent. Wit. to consent, Elbert Moseley and John Moseley. Sur. Robert Pollard, who testifies Jane is of age. Married 11 August by Rev. John Pollard. p. C-5

11 December 1786. COOPER, John and Mary Elizabeth Royall, who writes her own consent to John L. Cooper. Wit. to consent, John Townes, Junr. and Edmund Cooper. Sur. John Townes, Junr. p. C-2

22 December 1815. COOPER, William and Nancy Holt. Allen Jeter, her Guardian, consents. Wit. to consent, Joel Morris and John Roberts. Sur. Joel Morris. p. C-5

29 August 1808. COSBY, Jeremiah and Betsy Ennis, dau. of Rice Ennis. Sur. David Johnson. Married 1 September by Rev. Zachariah G. Leigh. p. C-4

12 June 1809. COUSINS, John C. and Elizabeth Allen, dau. of William Allen. Sur. Thomas Woodward. p. C-4

17 March 1811. COUSINS, Robert and Sally Allen, dau. of Sam'l Allen, who consents. Wit. to consent, Alexander Allen. Sur. Alezander Allen. p. C-5

29 July 1775. COX, Henry and Elizabeth Chappell, of Raleigh Parish. Sur. James Chappell. Henry Cox is of Chesterfield County. p. C-2

21 November 1764. COX, Matthew and Mary Bagley, dau, of George Bagley, who consents. Wit. to consent, Rolfe Eldridge. Sur. James Bagley. p. C-1

25 June 1799. CRADDOCK, Asa and Polly Harper, dau. of John Harper, Sr. Sur. John Harper. Married 25 June by Rev. John Skurrey. p. C-4

27 April 1775. CRADDOCK, Charles and Rebecca Clough, both of Raleigh Parish. Sur. Thomas Jones. p. C-2

12 February 1799. CRADDOCK, Claiborne and Mary Robertson. Sur. Nathan Robertson. Married 12 February by Rev. John Skurrey. p. C-4

4 February 1780. CRADDOCK, David and Elizabeth Bagley, of Nottoway Parish. Sur. Anderson Bagley. p. C-2

7 October 1806. CRADDOCK, James and Judith Robertson. Sur. Claiborne Craddock. Married 9 October by Rev. John Skurrey. p. C-4

28 July 1763. CRADDOCK, Richard and Elizabeth Hill, spinster. Sur. James Hill. p. C-1

20 May 1780. CRADDOCK, William and Elizabeth Scott, dau. of B____ Scott, who consents. Sur. Daniel Jones. William is son of John Craddock, who consents. p. C-2

15 December 1791. CRADDOCK, William and Sarah Truly, dau. of John Truly. Sur. John Townes, Jr. Married by Rev. John Brunskill. p. C-4

25 September 1786. CRAGHEAD, George and Pretonella (?) Lamkin, dau. of Peter Lamkin. Sur. Sharpe Lamkin. p. C-2

15 May 1766. CRANE, John and Mary Lewelling. Sur. Alexander Lewelling. p. C-1
"This is to certify to you that bans of Marriage between John Crane and Mary Lewelling has been thrice published In Nottoway Parrish. Wit my hand this 11 day of May 1766." Signed: "Thos. Payne."
"P. S. The reason why I give this Certificate Mr. Wilkerson is gone from home and before he went away he delivered his papers up to me as they might be published In Due time and Desired me to give Certificate to those that required them and he would answer the same as under his own hand." Signed: "Thos. Payne."

3 January 1786. CRENSHAW, Anthony and Mason Jeter, who writes her own consent. Wit. to consent, Christian Winston and Benjamin Hobson. Sur. David Crenshaw. Married 7 January by Rev. Arch^d W. Roberts, of Prince Edward Co. p. C-2

28 January 1780. CRENSHAW, David and Elizabeth Smith. Samuel Smith gives "my full consent." Sur. Burwell Smith. (He signs:"Burrel.") p. C-2

25 April 1785. CRITCHER, Thomas and Jean Jinkins, dau. of J. S. Jinkins, who consents. Sur. Davis Booker. p. C-2

26 September 1765. CROSS, John and Elizabeth Cocke, who writes her own consent. Wit. to consent, Abraham Cocke and Stephen Cocke. Sur. Stephen Cocke. p. C-1

22 August 1789. CROWDER, Abraham and Mary Worsham. Her Guardian, Burrel (Burwell?) Coleman, consents. Wit. to consent, James Bevill and William Adams. Sur. Abraham Burton. Married 25 August by Rev. Robert Marshall. p. C-3

6 November 1785. CROWDER, Drury and Susanna Young, who writes her own consent. Sur. Robert Powell. p. C-2

12 December 1785. CROWDER, Herbert and Molley Watson, dau. of Jesse Watson, who consents. Sur. Robert Winfree. Married by Rev. Simeon Walton. p. C-2

25 May 1795. CROWDER, Herod Tucker and Frances Burton, dau. of Abel Burton. Sur. John Southall. p. C-5

1 September 1810. CROWDER, Herod T. and Eliza Smith. John Neal requests this license and says Elizabeth. Wit. to request, John Lee and Thomas Neal. Sur. Thomas Neal. p. C-5

11 July 1785. CROWDER, John and Ann Crowder, dau. of William Crowder, who consents. Wit. to consent, Reuben Jones. Sur. Ambrose Jeter. p. C-2

5 November 1794. CROWDER, John M. and Elizabeth Webster, dau. of Anthony Webster. Sur. Thos. Webster. Married 13 November by Rev. James McGlasson. p. C-4

11 July 1764. CROWDER, William and Ann Marshall. William Marshall consents. Sur. Robert Marshall. p. C-1

21 October 1810. CRUTE, Clemmonds and Sally Miller, dau. of Dabney Miller. Sur. Geo. C. Moore. p. C-5 (His name has been given as Clemends and Clements - Clemmonds is in the bond.)

27 October 1785. CRUTE, John Lumpkin and Rebecca Smith, dau. of Samuel Smith, who consents. Wit. to consent, Dan¹ Verser and Robt. Jones. Sur. William Smith. Married by Rev. Simeon Walton. p. C-2

15 November 1779. CRUTE, Robert and Susanna Lamkin.
Sur. Stith Hardaway. p. C-2

11 February 1800. DABBS, William and Polly Foster.
Sur. John Foster. p. D-2

27 September 1809. DANIEL, Stephen and Mary Willis.
Sur. Anthony Smith. Married 28 September by Rev.
Zachariah G. Leigh. p. D-2

-- May 1751. DANIEL, William and Agnes Markha-. Sur.
Francis McCraw. p. D-1 (Bond is mutilated.)

2 January 1783. DAVENPORT, William and Mary Nunnally.
Sur. George Grizzle. Wit. to bond, Peter Lamkin, Junr.
p. D-1

11 September 1769. DAVIDSON, George and Brazelear
Atkins, who writes her own consent. Wit. to consent,
James Atkins and William Atkins. Sur. John Forsith
Smith. George Davidson is of Prince Edward County.
p. D-1

24 September 1784. DAVIS, Asa and Frances Lipscomb, dau.
of Uriah Lipscomb, who consents. Wit. to consent,
Charles Winfree and Benj. Lipscomb. Sur. Gresset Davis.
p. D-1

22 February 1781. DAVIS, Hezekiah and Jencey Phillips.
Sur. Medkif Thompson. p. D-1

28 February 1783. DAVIS, John and Hannah Clough, dau. of
Eliza Clough. Sur. Charles Craddock. John Townes, Guardian of John Davis, consents, 28 February 1783. Wit. to
consent, Eliza Clough, Senr. and John Townes, Senr. p. D-1

-- ----- -----. DAVIS, John and Sophia Barns. Married by
Rev. S. Walton. In: "List, Since October 1787." Minister's Return.

24 March 1808. DEAREN, Rowlett and Jane Allen. Sur. Samuel Allen. Married by Rev. John Skurrey. p. D-2

27 December 1804. DEARING, Daniel and Anna Mitchell.
J. C. Mitchell consents. Wit. to consent, Moses Mitch-
ell and Polley Mitchell, "mother of the daughter."
Sur. Coleman Wills. p. D-2

28 November 1814. DEARING, William and Elizabeth Dickerson, who writes her own consent to William Dearen. Wit.
to consent, William Mottley and John A. Dalby. Sur. William Mottley. Married 28 November by Rev. John Skurrey,
who says William Dearen. p. D-2

18 December 1799. DEATON, Elijah and Nancy Pollard, dau.
of Leacher (?) Pollard, who consents. Wit. to consent,
Thomas Pollard and James Lovern. Sur. Thomas Pollard.
Married 19 December by Rev. John Pollard. p. D-2

12 May 1756. DEATON, James and Obedience Jackson. Sur.
Mathew Jackson. p. D-1

3 December 1800. DEATON, James and Elizabeth Pollard,
dau. of Robert Pollard, who consents. Wit. to consent,
Leah Pollard and Thomas Pollard. Sur. Thomas Pollard.
Married 5 December by Rev. John Pollard. p. D-2

23 December 1801. DEATON, John and Mary C. Jones. Sur.
Richd C. Craddock. p. D-2

16 April 1808. DEATON, Levi and Elizabeth P. Mitchell,
dau. of John Mitchell, who consents. Wit. to consent,
Anderson H. Jones and Polley R. Mitchell. Sur. Anderson H. Jones. Married 19 April by Rev. John Skurrey.
p. D-2

13 December 1803. DEATON, William and Mary Rowlett Traylor. Sur. Edmund Webster. Married 13 December by Rev.
John Pollard. p. D-2

23 May 1807. DELANEY, David and Nancy Belcher, dau. of
Mary Belcher. Sur. John Sudberry. Married 23 May by
Rev. William Dier. p. D-2

16 October 1786. DELANEY, William and Martha Munford.
Sur. John Munford. p. D-1

4 August 1801. DEMOVILL, Griffin and Phoebe Foster,
dau. of Richard Foster, who consents. Wit. to consent,
Elizabeth Meredith and Austin Noble. Sur. Austin Noble.
Married 5 August by Rev. John Skurrey. p. D-2

6 September 1803. DENNIS, Francis and Nancy E. Roberts,
dau. of P. (?) Roberts, who consents. His consent says
Francis Dennis is of Nottoway County. Wit. to consent,
Richd Hyde and Chastain Roberts. Sur. Chastain Roberts.
p. D-2

20 October 1764. DENNIS, Richard, Jr. and Martha Haskins. Sur. Charles Haskins. p. D-1

1 December 1786. DICKEN, Thomas and Elizabeth Smith.
Elizabeth M. Smith consents. Wit. to consent, Thos.
Morris, Fanney Scott and Agnes Smith. Sur. Richard
Smith. Married by Rev. Charles Anderson. p. D-1

34

26 December 1780. DICKENSON, Naton and Mary Foster.
Sur. Millinton Roach. p. D-1

13 October 1786. DICKEY, Robert and Mary French, dau.
of Mary French, who consents. Consent addressed: "To
any Minister of the Gospel." Sur. Abraham Dunnavant.
p. D-1

19 October 1786. DICKEY, Robert and Rebecca Coleman
French. Request for this license is made by Mary
French. Wit. to request, Charles Featherston and Ann
Featherston. Sur. Abraham Dunnavant. (Both bonds are
in the same bundle.) This marriage is NOT in the Regis-
ter.

Dier - Dyer

19 January 1792. DYER, Daniel and Prudence Ann Crittington, granddaughter of Henry Crittington, who consents. Sur. John L. Cooper. Wit. to bond, John Johnson. p. D-2
(Daniel signs Dier.)

24 September 1803. DIER, John and Elizabeth Sadler.
Sur. Samuel Allen. Married 25 September by Rev. William Dier. p. D-2

24 November 1808. DIER, Thomas and Mary Belcher. Sur.
Instance Hall. p. D-2

29 January 1797. DYER, William and Prudence Ann Cad-
tington (?). Sur. William Mann. p. D-2

11 December 1786. DOUGLAS, William and Martha Taylor
Selden. Sur. Francis Fitzgerald. p. D-1

17 July 1786. DOWDY, Richard and Martha Eans, dau. of
Alex C. Fowler, who consents. Wit. to consent, Sherwood Fowler and Edmund Fowler. Sur. Henry Eans. p. D-1

1 October 1804. DOYEAL, John and Polley Seay. Sur.
William Thompson. p. D-2

18 June 1798. DRAKE, Elisha and Dolly Perdue. Sur.
George Ballard. p. D-2

26 February 1807. DRAKE, Francis and Polly Farley.
Sur. Thos: Worsham. p. D-2

22 February 1790. DRAKE, James and Prudence Archer Hastings. Sary Hastings writes that Prudence "is of age to
marry." Wit. to consent, Robert Crowder and Giney Raglin. Sur. Sutten Hastings. p. D-1

23 November 1809. DRAKE, James W. and Polly Tanner. Sur. Eleazer Coleman. Married 26 November by Rev. James Chappell. p. D-2

25 July 1805. DRAKE, Pleasant and Martha Hastings, dau. of Elizabeth Hastings. Sur. Thos: Worsham. p. D-2

28 August 1783. DRAKE, Thomas, Jr. and Elizabeth Truit. Sur. Thomas Drake. p. D-1

23 February 1767. DUDLEY, Thomas and Milly Lea, of Nottoway Parish, dau. of William Lea, who consents. Wit. to consent, Andrew Lea and Lucey Lea. Sur. Andrew Lea. p. D-1

22 January 1790. DUNAWAY, Charles and Dicy Clay, dau. of Ann Clay, who consents. Wit. to consent, Bachelder Graves and Thomas Clay. Sur. Bachelder Graves. Married 26 January by Rev. Robert Marshall, who says Charles Dunnaway, Planter. p. D-1

5 August 1790. DUNCAN, Robert and Sarah Drake. Sur. Thomas Drake. Married 8 August by Rev. Robert Marshall, who says Robert Duncan, Planter. p. D-1

15 April 1785. DUNNAVANT, Abner and Phebe Worsham, dau. of Henry Worsham, who consents. Wit. to consent, John Childress, who is surety. p. D-1

27 November 1787. DUNNAVANT, Daniel and Rhody Gordon, who writes her own consent. Wit. to consent, R. C. Dickey and Elizabeth A____. Sur. Robert Dickey. Married by Rev. John Brunskill. p. D-1

29 July 1788. DUNNAVANT, Frederick and Patsy Tatum Bevill. Robert Bevill consents. Wit. to consent, Clayborn Bevill and Abraham Crowder. Sur. Thomas Murray. p. D-1

23 October 1782. DUNNA____, Philip and Martha Dun_____. Sur. Hodges Dun_____. (Dunnavant?). (Bond mutilated.) p. D-1

20 June 1797. DUNNAVANT, Philip and Ann Dunnavant. Sur. William Booker. p. D-2

25 September 1788. DUNNAVANT, Thomas and Jelusha Crittenton, dau. of Henry Crittenton, who consents. Wit. to consent, Philip Dunnavant and Ans. Hurt. Sur. Anderson Hurt. p. D-1

27 July 1780. DUNNAVANT, William and Susanna Pemberton Smith. Sur. Hodges Dunnavant. p. D-1

10 September 1808. DUNNAVANT, William and Elizabeth Worsham, dau. of James Worsham, who consents. Wit. to consent, Daniel Bell and George Bell. Sur. David Bell. Married 17 September by Rev. John Skurrey. p. D-2

20 December 1783. DUPUY, James, Sr. and Prudence Wills. Sur. Laurence Wills. p. D-1

25 September 1765. DUPUY, John B. and Mary Ford, of Raleigh Parish. Sur. Christopher Ford. p. D-1

16 July 1739. DURWIN, Nicholas and Elizabeth Jones. Sur. John Jones. p. D-1
Will Book I, p. 48 - Will of John Jones, of Raleigh Parish, Amelia Co., names, among others, wife Mary and daughter Elizabeth, wife of Nicholas Durwin.

2 June 1783. EAGLE, Edward and Mary Lovern, who writes her own consent. Mary Lovern, her mother testifies Mary is over 21. Sur. Ambrose Jeter. p. E-1

26 February 1789. ENES (Eanes?), Henry and Mary Hanson, who writes her own consent to Henry Eanes. Wit. to consent, Will: Fagg and Joshua Hunly. Sur. William Fagg. p. E-1

4 February 1805. EANS, Henry P. and Nancy C. Booker. Her Guardian is Jacob Roberts. Sur. Joe Hillsman. Married 8 February by Rev. John Skurrey. p. E-2

2 July 1805. EANS, Herbert and Rebecca Crowder. Sur. Allen Jeter, who testifies Rebecca is 21. Married 5 July by Rev. John Pollard. p. E-2

22 December 1787. ECKLES, Edward and Betsy Tucker, dau. of Mathew Tucker, who consents. Sur. Paschal Tucker. p. E-1
Was this a double wedding? See Paschal Tucker.

13 November 1786. ECKLES, Isham and Philadelphia Tucker, dau. of Matt Tucker. "License by request of Matt Tucker, her father." Sur. Mat Tucker. p. E-1

27 February 1789. ECKLES, Joel and Polly Eckles, dau. of Thomas Eckles, who consents. Wit. to consent, Edward Eckles and Paschal Tucker. Sur. Edward Eckles. p. E-1

20 August 1783. ECOLS, Elkanah and Elizabeth Anderson. Sur. Richard Anderson. p. E-1

29 November 1803. EDMUNDS, John and Eliza Randolph, dau. of William Randolph. Sur. Bathurst Randolph. p. E-2

13 June 1789. EDMUNDS, William and Susanna Hood. Sur.
Solomon Hood. p. E-1

27 June 1783. EDWARDS, Jacob and Nancy Hudson. Sur.
Ellison Young. p. E-1

9 June 1795. EDWARDS, Peter and Frances Park Jeter.
Thomas Elmore is her Guardian. Sur. John Hannah. p. E-2

7 September 1795. EGGLESTON, Edmund and Jane Segar Lang-
horne. Her Guardian, Richard Eggleston, consents. Sur.
Samuel Farrar. p. E-2

26 December 1807. EGGLESTON, Edward and Judith Booker.
Sur. Daniel Booker. Married 27 December by Rev. Zachariah G. Leigh. p. E-2

25 November 1790. EGGLESTON, George and Elizabeth Macon,
whose Guardian, Jacob Williamson, consents. Wit. to consent, John Wild (?) and Thomas Meeks. Sur. John Townes.
p. E-1

17 October 1776. EGGLESTON, Joseph and Judith Bentley,
widow, of Nottoway Parish. Sur. Archibald M. Roberts.
Wit. to bond, Judith Moulson and Mary Eggleston. p. E-1

25 February 1788. EGGLESTON, Joseph and Sally Meade,
dau. of E. Meade, whose consent says, Major Joseph
Eggleston. Sur. John Archer. p. E-1

7 May 1796. EGGLESTON, Joseph and Judith Cary Eggleston. Sur. Edward Eggleston. Wit. to bond, R^d Eggleston. p. E-2

1 November 1783. EGGLESTON, Richard and Judith Moulson.
Sur. Thos: Mumford, Jr. p. E-1
(Note: Register says 2 June - bond says 1 November.)

25 October 1806. EGGLESTON, Richard and Anne Hill.
Sur. Edward Eggleston. Married 28 October by Rev. John
Skurrey. p. E-2

2 May 1812. EGGLESTON, Richard and Martha Baugh, who
writes her own consent. Sur. Edward Eggleston. Married
5 May by Rev. Conrad Speece. p. E-2

23 December 1800. EGGLESTON, William T. and Martha
Cocke. Sur. James Cocke. p. E-2

2 January 1788. EGMON, Lott and Judah Roberts, dau. of
Step. Roberts, who consents. Wit. to consent, John Fos-
ter and Lucy Foster. Sur. John Foster. p. E-1
(Register says Egsmond - bond and consent say Egmon.)

15 Settember 1778. ELAM, Barkley and Mary Israel Willson.
Sur. William Hall. p. E-1
William Hall, in his consent, 15 September 1778, says that
Mary Israel Willson is his granddaughter and lives with
him; that she is daughter of John Wilson of Mecklenburg
County and that Barkley Elam is of Chesterfield County.
(Note and bond are dated 15 September.)

10 September 1792. ELAM, Essex and Lavinia Crowder. Sur.
Lodowick Elam. Married 15 September by Rev. Walthall
Robertson. p. E-2

2 May 1791. Elam, Lodwick and Judith Blackwell Powell,
dau. of John Powell, who requests this license. Wit. to
request, Abraham Powell and Daniel Wilkerson. Sur. Abraham Powell. p. E-1
(Bond and request for license have the same date.)

31 August 1811. ELAM, Miles and Lucy Talley, dau. of
Patron Talley, whose request for this license says Lucy
is of age. Wit. to request, William Jannet and Grief
Powell. Sur. David Talley. p. E-2

27 October 1785. ELLINGTON, David and Mary Malone
Dupuy. Sur. Peter Dupuy. p. E-1

14 November 1786. ELLINGTON, Grief and Jane Hall, dau.
of Daniel Hall. Sur. Daniel Tucker. p. E-1

10 December 1802. ELLINGTON, Joel and Mary Webber.
Sur. Jesse Bryant. Married by Rev. John Pollard. p. E-2

9 November 1763. ELLIS, Ellyson and Mary Zachary. Sur.
Bartholomew Zachary. Wit. to bond, Rolfe Eldridge.
p. E-1

20 March 1806. ELLIS, James and Rachel Morris, dau. of
Zachariah Morris. Married 20 March by Rev. John
Skurrey. p. E-2

9 November 1754. ELLIS, Richard and Mary Cocke, dau. of
Abraham Cocke, Senr. Sur. William Watkins, Junr. Wit.
to bond, Jonathan Gibson. p. E-1

6 January 1789. ELLIS, Thomas and Ann Ammonet, who
writes her own consent. Wit. to consent, Mary Weldon
Barkley, William Barkley and William Holmes, Clk. Sur.
William Barkley. p. E-1

28 March 1789. ELLIS, Wm. Cocke and Mary Cocke. Sur.
Stephen Cocke. p. E-1

8 March 1756. ELLYSON, Gerrard and Elizabeth Ford,
widow. Sur. Francis Clement. p. E-1

4 July 1782. ELMORE, Thomas and Letticia Williams, dau.
of Philip Williams, who consents. Wit. to consent, Pleasant Roberts and Zachariah Compton. Sur. Charles Old.
p. E-1   (Is Letitia correct?)

22 July 1802. EPES, Francis and Amey Willson, dau. of
Mary Willson. Sur. Paschal Perdue. p. E-2

22 January 1793. EPPS, John and Martha Allen, dau. of
David Allen. Sur. David Allen, Jr. Married 26 January
by Rev. Robert Walthall, who says John Eppes, Planter.
p. E-2

23 December 1788. EPES, Thomas and Catharine Williams,
dau. of Thomas Williams, who consents. Wit. to consent,
W. Greenhill and Elizabeth Williams. Sur. Philip W.
Greenhill. p. E-1

25 August 1814. EPPES, Thomas and Frances B. Jones, who
writes her own consent. Sur. Samuel Scott. Married 1
September by Rev. James Chappell. p. E-2

27 April 1758. ERSKINE, Alexr. and Sarah Wallsen, spinster. Sur. Thomas Claiborne. p. E-1
(The bond has Wallsen - should this be Watson?)

24 May 1787. ESTES, Henry and Elizabeth Atkinson, dau.
of Thomas Atkinson, who consents. Wit. to consent,
John L. Crute and Benj: Overton. Sur. Benj: Overton.
p. E-1

14 December 1785. EVANS, Ellis and Mary Gunn, dau. of
Thomas Gunn, who consents. Sur. John Evans. Married by
Rev. Simeon Walton. p. E-1

11 December 1815. EVANS, German and Sally Hood, whose
Guardian, James Allen, requests this license. Wit. to
request, Bernard Southall, who is surety. Married 13
December by Rev. James Chappell. p. E-2

29 June 1781 (87?). EVANS, John and Ann Irby. Sur. John
Irby. p. E-1

23 November 1764. EVANS, Stephen, Jr. and Obedience
Ellington, dau. of Daniel Ellington, who consents. Wit.
to consent, George Cabiness and Cabiness Ellington. Sur.
George Cabiness. p. E-1

1 February 1781. FAGG, William and Martha Mayes, dau. of Phebe Mayes, who consents "as mother and Guardian." Wit. to consent, Matthew Robertson and Bartholomew Vaughan. Sur. Mathew Robertson. p. F-1

9 February 1790. FAGG, William and Mary Ford, who writes her own consent. Wit. to consent, Francis Barnes and Salle Barnes. Sur. Francis Barnes. p. F-2

28 September 1786. FARLEY, Daniel and Martha Pryor, who writes her own consent. Wit. to consent, Abraham Hatchett and Grief Talley. Sur. Grief Talley. p. F-2

10 February 1807. FARLEY, Henry and Tabitha Holt, dau. of Richard Holt, who consents. Wit. to consent, Stephen Farley and Pleasant Rucker. Sur. Wm. Farley. Married 12 February by Rev. John Skurrey. p. F-3

27 November 1788. FARLEY, John and Elizabeth Simmons Stott, dau. of James Stott, who consents. Sur. James Farley. p. F-2   (Bond mutilated.)

27 January 1778. FARLEY, Nathaniel and Sarah Farley, dau. of James Farley, whose consent is dated 26 January 1778. Wit. to consent, Francis Farley and Maryan Farley. Sur. Henry Farley. p. F-1

5 November 1809. FARLEY, Peter and Mary Bowman. Sur. William Dearing. Married 9 November by Rev. John Pollard. p. F-2

27 December 1787. FARLEY, Stephen and Mary Mitchell, niece of Charles Stewart, who consents. Wit. to consent, John Farley and Arch^d Farley. Sur. James Mann. Married by Rev. S. Walton. p. F-2

17 August 1812. FARLEY, Stephen and Elizabeth P. Allen, dau. of Richard Allen, of Nottoway County, who consents. Wit. to consent, Edward Farley and Edmund Morris. Sur. Edmund Morris. Married 20 August by Rev. John Skurrey. p. F-3

24 May 1787. FARMER, Absalom and Gracy Booker. Sur. Henry Estes. p. F-2

26 November 1761. FARMER, Francis and Mary Ferguson. Sur. John Ferguson. p. F-1

14 June 1784. FARMER, Lodwick and Frances Brooks. Sur. William Brooks. p. F-1

28 March 1776. FARMER, Stephen and Elizabeth Anderson, dau. of John Anderson, who is surety. p. F-1

25 November 1790. FARRAR, Samuel and Eliza Eggleston.
Sur. Richard Eggleston. p. F-2

3 November 1788. FARISS, Joel and Jane Hall, who writes
her own consent. Wit. to consent, Stephen Hall and
Peter Ellington. Sur. Peter Ellington. p. F-2

13 June 1815. FARRISS, Marshall B. and Rhoda Morris,
dau. of John Morris, who consents. Wit. to consent,
John Morris, Jr. and John D. Angel. Sur. John Morris,
Jr. p. F-3

11 ----- ----. FEASTON, William and Catherine Neal.
Sur. Roger Thomson. p. F-1   (A mutilated bond.)

23 November 1781. FEATHERSTONE, Charles and Ann French.
Sur. Thomas French. p. F-1

21 April 1789. FARGUSON, John and Olive Williams. Sur.
Burwell Jackson. Peleg Farguson consents. Wit. to his
consent, Burwell Jackson. p. F-2

9 April 1760. FERGUSON, Robert and Martha Foster. Sur.
Robert Ferguson, Jr. p. F-1

23 April 1789. FERGUSON, Robert and Sarah Stewart, who
writes her own consent. Wit. to consent, Milton Ford and
A. C. Overton. Sur. Milton Ford. p. F-2

24 February 1785. FINNEY, John and Sarah Chappell. Sur.
Cain Mann. p. F-1

10 March 1797. FINNEY, John and Nancy Garland. Sur.
Miles C. Finney. p. F-3

5 January 1801. FISHER, William and Anny Foster. Sur.
Richard Foster. Married 5 January by Rev. John Pollard.
p. F-2   (Both bond and Minister say Anny.)

26 July 1808. FISHER, William and Mary Holt. Sur.
David Holt. Married 27 July by Rev. John Pollard.
p. F-2

14 January 1786. FITZ GERALD, Francis and Mary Eppes,
dau of Fran: Eppes, who consents. Sur. Stith Hardaway.
p. F-2

5 December 1783. FLEET, William and Sarah Meeks. Married by Rev. Charles Anderson. Minister's Return.

18 November 1788. FLETCHER, James and Rebecca Fletcher.
Sur. Nathan Fletcher, Jr. p. F-2

10 November 1785. FLETCHER, Richard and Nancy Fletcher, dau. of Nathan Fletcher, who consents and is surety. p. F-1

23 December 1796. FLUSHING, Mayes and Nancy Johnson. Sur. Bennett Johnson. p. F-2

5 September 1795. FORD, Charles and Betse Chaffin, dau. of Joshua Chaffin. Sur. John Chaffin. p. F-3

1 September 1786. FORD, Daniel and Rebecca Hawks, who writes her own consent. Wit. to consent, John Hawks and Joshua Hawks. Sur. John Hawkes. p. F-2

6 November 1780. FORD, George and Martha Hawkins. Sur. Martin Chandler. p. F-1
(George signs the bond, George Foard.)

28 December 1797. FORD, Hezekiah and Nancy Muse. Her Guardian is William Wood. Sur. Wm. Robertson. p. F-2

4 April 1791. FORD, Samuel and Martha Booker. Sur. James Howlett. p. F-2

31 March 1756. FOREST, George and Frances Atwood, dau. of James Atwood, who consents. Wit. to consent, John Forest and Joshua Gilliam. Sur. Richard Atwood. p. F-1

19 December 1787. FORREST, John and Martha Womack, dau. of Thomas Womack, who is surety. p. F-2

19 September 1765. FORREST, Richard and Elizabeth Oliver, of Nottoway Parish, dau. of James Oliver, who consents. Wit. to consent, John Morrison and Richard Forrest. Sur. John Thomson. p. F-1

7 September 1762. FORSE, John and Jean Gordon. Sur. James Henderson. p. F-1

7 August 1781. FOSTER, Abner and Drusilla O Neal. Married by Rev. Jeremiah Walker. Minister's Return.

18 November 1784. FOSTER, Achilles and Rebecca Walthall. Sur. Daniel Walthall. p. F-1

22 December 1781. FOSTER, Anthony and Elizabeth Asselin. Sur. Thos: Asselin. p. F-1

21 December 1807. FOSTER, Asey and Martha Hudson. Her Guardian, Joshua Smithey, consents. Sur. Pleasant Seay. Married 22 December by Rev. John Pollard, who also says, Asey Foster. p. F-3

6 November 1789. FOSTER, George and Elizabeth Foster, who writes her own consent. Wit. to consent, Thos. Jones and Edward Jones. Sur. Edward Jones. p. F-2

24 May 1788. FOSTER, Joel and Edie Amos. Sur. James Amos. p. F-2

28 July 1800. FOSTER, Joel and Elizabeth Hill, dau. of Sarah Lockett. Sur. Robert Craddock. p. F-2

6 January 1809. FOSTER, Joseph and Elizabeth Wright. Guardian: "Signed by John Jeter." Sur. Henry Haskew. Married 8 January by Rev. John Pollard. p. F-2

9 December 1812. FOSTER, Josiah and Obedience E. Mitchell, whose Guardian is John Mitchell and he is surety. Married 17 December by Rev. John Skurrey. p. F-3

10 June 1775. FOSTER, Richard and Judith Walker, of Raleigh Parish, who writes her own consent. Sur. Edmund Walker. Richard Foster is of Hanover County. p. F-1

13 March 1793. FOSTER, Richard and Obedience Green. Sur. John Townes. Richard Foster is of Prince Edward County. p. F-3

24 September 1799. FOSTER, Richard and Lucy Allen, dau. of Richard Allen. Sur. Thomas Meader. Married 26 September by Rev. John Skurrey. p. F-3

12 February 1781. FOSTER, Robert and Mary Forest. Sur. Josiah Forrest. p. F-1

20 December 1781. FOSTER, Robert and Elizabeth Jones, sister of Daniel Jones, who writes permission for this license to be issued and he is surety. p. F-1

27 January 1807. FOSTER, Robert and Nancy H. Mitchell, dau. of John Mitchell. Sur. John Foster. Married 29 January by Rev. John Skurrey. p. F-3

6 October 1779. FOSTER, William and Elizabeth Hastings. Sur. Robert Gilliam. p. F-1

17 July 1781. FOSTER, William and Mary Ann James, widow. Sur. Richard Ananson. (Anderson?). p. F-1

15 June 1784. FOWLER, Edmund and Sarah Clements. Sur. Henry Walden. p. F-1

25 June 1782. FOWLER, Sherwood and Mary Wingo, dau. of John Wingo, who consents. Wit. to consent, John Wingo and Monet Wingo. Sur. John Wingo. p. F-1

11 January 1768. FOWLKES, (Folks), Daniel and Lucretia
Brown, of Raleigh Parish, who writes her own consent.
Wit. to consent, Alexander Brown and Joel Jackson. Sur.
Joel Jackson. p. F-1
(Consent has Joel Folks.).

2 March 1782. Fowlkes, Henry and Tabitha Bass. Married
by Rev. Jeremiah Walker. Minister's Return.

23 November 1780. FOWLKES, James and Sally Foster, dau.
of Mary Foster, who consents. Sur. Jennings Fowlkes.
James is son of John Fowlkes of Amelia, who consents.
p. F-1

-- ----- ----. FOWLKES, John and Judith Pennix. Married by Rev. S. Walton. In a list "Since October 1787.
Minister's Return.

18 June 1787. FOWLKES, Joseph Jennings and Frances Bass,
dau. of John Bass, whose consent is dated 18 June, 1787
and says, "my Darter." Wit. to consent, Samuel Bruce
and Armstreet (?) Bruce. Sur. William Fowlkes. Married
by Rev. Simeon Walton. p. F-2

29 September 1792. FOWLKES, Joseph Jennings and Molly
Craddock. Sur. John Hill Craddock. p. F-2

26 August 1784. FOWLKES, Nathan and Nancy Bagley. Sur.
Ruler Richardson. p. F-1

22 February 1788. FOWLKES, Sterling and Elizabeth Jennings, dau. of James Jennings, who consents. Wit. to
consent, Wm. Pamplin and John "West Brook." Sur. William
Pamplin. Married by Rev. Simeon Walton. p. F-2

1 May 1802. FRANKLIN, Jesse and Rhody Claybrook. Sur.
William Burton. Married 1 May by Rev. John Skurrey.
p. F-3

8 September 1802. FRASER, William and Elizabeth Yeargain.
(Yeargan?) Sur. William Coleman. p. F-2

14 September 1781. FREEMAN, Anderson and Mildred Johnson.
Sur. Philip A. Johnson. p. F-1

10 August 1785. FREEMAN, Isham and Patty Bevill, dau. of
Joseph Bevill, who consents. Sur. Abraham Powell. p. F-1

27 July 1787. FREEMAN, John and Betsy Mitchell, dau. of
Evans Mitchell. Sur. Anderson Freeman. Married by Rev.
John Brunskill. p. F-2

27 April 1809. FREEMAN, John and "left out". Sur. John Freeman. Married 6 May by Rev. John Skurrey, who says John Freeman and Polly Bradley. p. F-3

18 July 1812. FRENCH, Micajah and Lucy Hogan. Sur. Samuel Williams, who testifies Lucy is "upwards of 21." p. F-3

13 December 1793. FUQUA, Samuel and Prudence Ford. John Wily, her Guardian, consents. Wit. to consent, Wm. Archer and Joel Ward. Sur. William Robertson. Married 14 December by Rev. John Pollard. p. F-3

11 December 1792. FUQUA, William and Frankey Dunnavant, dau. of Abraham Dunnavant. Sur. Edward Driver. p. F-3

16 April 1787. GARLAND, John and Nancy Crawley, sister of David Crawley, who is her Guardian and he consents. Wit. to consent, John Crawley and Jno. Jones. Sur. Is. Holmes. John Garland is of Hanover County. p. G-1

3 September 1798. GARRETT, Samuel and Elizabeth Braughton. Sur. John Braughton. p. G-2

22 September 1774. GATES, James and Obedience Walthall. Sur. Christopher Walthall. p. G-1

-- ----- ----. GAULDIN (?), William and Elizabeth Angel. Married by Rev. John Pollard "since August Court 1789." Minister's Return.

14 January 1783. GAY, William and Judith Scott, dau. of John Scott, "late of Amelia County." George Carrington, her Guardian, consents. Wit. to consent, N. Carrington, William B------ and -------- Carrington. Sur. Thomas Mumford, Junr. p. G-1

13 September 1809. GENT, Peter and Martha Worsham, dau. of Archer Worsham. Sur. William C. Bass. p. G-2

2 November 1778. GIBBS, Edward and Martha Dunnavant. Sur. Philip Dunnavant. p. G-1

15 September 1813. GIBBS, Thomas and Elizabeth A. Hall, dau. of William Hall, who consents. Wit. to consent, Miles Archer and Eliza P. Parham. Sur. Miles Archer. p. G-2

8 April 1769. GIBBS, William and Elizabeth Webster. Sur. John Deaton. p. G-1

23 December 1786. GEFFORD, Joseph and Mary Powell, dau. of John Powell, who consents. Wit. to consent, Abram Powell and Robert Powell. Sur. Abraham Anderson. Married by Rev. John Brunskill, who says Joseph Gifford. p. G-1

28 June 1746. GILES, William and Mary Mattock Ellis, spinster. Sur. John Ellis. p. G-1

26 April 1787. GILES, William and Rebecca Walker Macon. Sur. Edmund Walker. p. G-1

6 March 1797. GILES, William B. and Martha Peyton Tabb, dau. of John Tabb. Sur. William M. Booker. p. G-2

22 October 1807. GILLS, Anderson and Polly Woodson, dau. of Joseph Woodson, who is surety. Married 27 October by Rev. Thomas Pettus. p. G-1

28 August 1810. GILLS, James and Nancy S. Woodson, dau. of Joseph Woodson, Jr., who consents. Wit. to consent, Robert J. Woodson and Susanna H. Clement. Sur. Robert J. Woodson. Married 30 August by Rev. John Pollard. p. G-2

11 March 1786. GILLS, John and Tabitha Anderson Jeter, dau. of Ambrose Jeter, who consents. Wit. to consent, Reubin Wright. Sur. William Pollard. p. G-1

6 March 1813. GILLS, Pleasant and Nancy Fowlkes. Her Guardian, Edward Claybrook, consents and he is surety. Married 11 March by Rev. John Skurrey. p. G-2

21 November 1767. GOOCH, John and Judith Redford, of Raleigh Parish. Sur. Francis Jackson. p. G-1

28 November 1769. GOOCH, William and Henrietta Maria Irby, both of Nottoway Parish. Charles Irby testifies she is daughter of Charles Irby, deceased, late of Amelia County, and that she is 21. Wit. to above, Susanah Irby and Susanah Cocke. Sur. Mason Piles. Wit. to bond, Rich'd Jones, Jr. p. G-1

1 December 1804. GOODE, Gaines and Ann Goode. Sur. Joseph Goode. Married 1 December by Rev. John Skurrey. p. G-2

20 April 1768. GOODE, Mackerness and Polly Anderson. Sur. Benjamin Walker. Mackerness Goode is of Prince Edward County. p. G-1

11 February 1793. GOODE, Philip, Jr. and Rebeckah Hayes,
dau. of Richard Hayes. Sur. James Hayes. p. G-2

15 November 1815. GOODE, Thomas and Fliza Royall Jones,
dau. of Ann Jones. Sur. William Mann. Married 16 November
by Rev. David Jones. p. G-2

2 April 1814. GOODWIN, David and Matilda Hill, dau. of
James Hill, whose consent says, "my daughter, Adaline
Matilda Hill." Wit. to consent, P. L. Townes and Edward
Hill. Sur. Edward Hill. Married 3 April by Rev. Zacha-
riah G. Leigh. p. G-2

12 January 1808. GOODWIN, Francis and Elizabeth Avery.
Sur. John Avery. p. G-2

18 June 1806. GOODWIN (Goodman?), James and Sally
Avery. Sur. Jacob Avery. p. G-2

6 May 1813. GOODWIN, Jesse and Nancy C. Roberts, dau.
of Jacob Roberts, who consents. Wit. to consent, John
Roberts and E. Tanner. Sur. John Roberts. Married 7
May by Rev. John Skurrey. p. G-2

14 January 1793. GRANT, William and Sally Tanner. Sur.
Robert Tanner. Married 18 January by Rev. Robert Walthall, who says William Grant, Planter, and Sarah Tanner. p. G-1

29 December 1803. GRANT, William and Martha Fagg. Married by Rev. John Skurrey. Minister's return. See Wilson Grant.

29 December 1803. GRANT, Wilson and Martha Fagg, who
writes her own consent to Wilson Grant. Wit. to consent, Richard Johnson and Charles Farmer. Sur. Richard Johnson, who testifies Martha is of age. p. G-2
See William Grant.

27 December 1803. GRAVES, Arthur and Fanny Eans, dau.
of Henry Eans, Sr. Sur. Dudley Seay. Married 28
December by Rev. John Skurrey. p. G-2

28 October 1784. GRAVES, Bachelor and Rhoda Clay. Sur.
Robert French. p. G-1

1 October 1809. GRAVES, Thomas and Susan Anderson.
Sur. Daniel Willson. p. G-2

5 September 1782. GRAY, Gabriel and Rebecca Willson.
Sur. Henry Walthall. Gabriel is son of John Gray, who
consents. Wit. to his consent, Peter Larkin, Junr. and
Henry Walthall. p. G-1

24 April 1777. GRAY, William and Susanna Crenshaw, of
Raleigh Parish, dau. of Mary Crenshaw, who consents.
Wit. to consent, David Crenshaw and Edm. Booker. Sur.
David Crenshaw. p. G-1

18 October 1781. GRAY, William and Lucy Willson. Sur.
Tom B. Willson. p. G-1

13 March 1793. GREEN, Abraham and Martha Armstead.
Sur. John Townes, Jr. p. G-2
(NOTE: This bond is in a package marked: "Bonds, 1792-
1809 - F to H." The Register says 1783.)

2 April 1799. GREEN, Caleb and Elizabeth Walden, dau. of
John Walden. Sur. David Crenshaw. Married 6 April 1799
by Rev. John Skurrey. p. G-2

24 August 1807. GREEN, Edward and Nancy M. Jeter, dau.
of Allen Jeter. Sur. Joseph Haskew. Married 26 August
by Rev. John Pollard. p. G-2

11 February 1813. GREENE, Herndon and Sally Johns. Her
Guardian, Daniel Verser, consents. Wit. to consent,
Booker Foster and Matilda Foster. Sur. Booker Foster.
Married 18 February by Rev. John Skurrey. p. G-2
(NOTE: This name is Greene on bond - Green, in consent.)

23 December 1788. GREEN, Jesse Davis and Martha Tanner,
dau. of Joel Tanner, Sr. She writes her own consent.
Wit. to consent, Mary Johns, R. Anderson and _____.
Sur. William Powell. Married 30 December by Rev. Thomas
Grymes. p. G-1

10 February 1768. GREEN, William and Obedience Obey
Green, of Raleigh Parish, dau. of Abraham Green, who is
surety. p. G-1

3 March 1804. GREEN, William and Nancy Bailey. Sur.
William Old. p. G-2

10 November 1768. GREENHILL, Paschal and Ann Ward,
orphan of Henry Ward. Lewellyn Jones, her Guardian,
consents. Wit. to consent, Will Watts and Luke Pryor.
Sur. Lewellyn Jones. p. G-1

24 June 1780. GREENHILL, William and Elizabeth Ward,
dau of Ben: Ward, who consents. Sur. Peter Randolph.
p. G-1

21 May 1813. GREGORY, William and Judith F. Willson,
dau. of Tom F. Willson, who consents. Wit. to consent,
J. Quarles and Roger Gregory. Sur. John Quarles. p. G-2

28 June 1787. GRIGGS, Charles and Eliza Mitchell. Sur.
William Cryer. p. G-1

13 February 1786. GRIZZLE, George and Sarah W. Sladen,
who writes her own consent. Wit. to consent, Jno. Royall
and Richd Pincham. Sur. Daniel Parham. p. G-1

28 April 1784. GUNN, Elisha and Rettis Wilkes, dau. of
John Wilkes, whose consent, dated 28 April, 1784, says,
"my daughter, Rittar." Wit. to consent, Willis Vaughan,
who is surety. p. G-1

1 December 1778. GUNN, Thomas and Sarah Davenport. Sur.
John Tucker, of Amelia County. p. G-1

11 January 1782. GUNN, Thomas and Ann Worsham. Sur.
William Osborne. p. G-1

21 January 1788. GUNN, William and Sally Black Cross.
Sur. Richard Cross. p. G-1

2 April 1790. HALL, Instance and Polly Archer, dau. of
Ann Archer, who consents. Wit. to consent, Wm. Wms.
Hall and Andrew Waugh. Sur. Wm. Wms. Hall. p. H-2

12 December 1800. HALL, John and Elizabeth Foster.
Sur. John Smith. Married 19 December by Rev. John Skurrey. p. H-3

12 November 1757. HAMLIN, Charles, Jr. and Agnes Cocke,
spinster. Abraham Cocke requests this license. Wit. to
request, Abra: Cocke, Jr. Sur. Samuel Sherwin. p. H-1

26 June 1788. HAMLIN, Daniel and Elizabeth Fowlkes, dau.
of Joseph Fowlkes, who consents. Wit. to consent, Sally
Fowlkes and Wm. Fowlkes. Sur. Benjamin Hawkins. Married
by Rev. S. Walton. p. H-2

22 December 1768. HAMLIN, John and Philadelphia Jones.
Wood Jones consents. Wit. to consent, Philip Jones and
Wood Jones. Sur. Richard Jones. p. H-1

26 January 1797. HANNAH, John and Sally W. Webster.
Sur. Charles Craddock. p. H-3

11 January 1768. HANSFORD, William and Janet Brown, who
writes her own consent. Wit. to consent, Alexander
Browne and Joel Jackson. Sur. Joel Jackson. William
Hansford is of Buckingham County. p. H-1

13 September 1774. HARDAWAY, Daniel and Ann Eggleston,
dau. of Jos: Eggleston, who consents. Wit. to consent,
William Jones and Stith Hardaway. Sur. William Jones.
p. H-1

29 August 1811. HARDAWAY, Daniel and Sarah T. Jones, dau. of Ann Jones, whose consent says, "to Dr. Daniel Hardaway." Wit. to consent, David Jones and Seth W. Jones. Sur. David C. Jones. p. H-4

5 December 1756. HARDAWAY, Stith and Purify Booker. Sur. John Booker. p. H-1

30 May 1767. HARDY, Covington and Catherine Beuford, "Buford." Sur. John Winn. p. H-1

"Since October 1787." HARPER, Daniel and Sally Griffin. Married by Rev. Charles Anderson. Minister's Return.

27 February 1782. HARPER, James and Mary Green. Marston Green consents. Wit. to consent, Francis Lee and Christiana Bennet. Sur. John Harper. p. H-2

27 March 1783. HARRIS, Benjamin and Martha Willson. Sur. Benjamin Moseley. p. H-2

"Since October 1787." HARRIS, John and Frances Trotter. Married by Rev. S. Walton. Minister's Return.

25 April 1814. HARRIS, John S. and Elizabeth P. Brackett, dau. of Ludwell Brackett, who consents. Wit. to consent, Benj. P. Howard and Thos. A. (H?) Walton. Sur. Benj. P. Howard. p. H-4

4 September 1787. HARRISON, William and Hannah Boggess, dau. of Henry Boggess, who consents. Sur. Burnett Boust (?). Married by Rev. Simeon Walton. p. H-2

3 October 1782. HARROLD, John and Martha Roberts. Married by Rev. Charles Anderson. Minister's Return.

22 April 1779. HARVEY, Thomas and Barbara Walton, of Nottoway Parish. Sur. Simeon Walton. Wit. to bond, Thos. I. Walton. Thomas is son of John Harvey, who consents. Wit. to his consent, Thos. Walton and Jesse Walton. p. H-1

18 April 1789. HARVEY, William and Agness Walton, dau. of Simon Walton, who consents. Wit. to consent, Edw. Craddock and William Bryan. Sur. Simon Walton. p. H-2

30 January 1808. HARVIE, Edwin and Martha Hardaway. Her Guardian is James Eggleston. Sur. Daniel Hardaway. p. H-3

26 December 1812. HASKEW, Henry and Elizabeth Crowder, who writes her own consent. Wit. to consent, Thomas W. Webster, who is surety. Married 27 December by Rev. John Skurrey. p. H-4

22 December 1807. HASKEW, Joseph and Elizabeth S. Foster, dau. of Anthony Foster, who consents. Wit. to consent, Joseph Foster and Lamkin Foster. Sur. Joseph Foster. Married by Rev. John Skurrey. p. H-3

25 November 1794. HASKINS, Creed and Martha C. Ogilby, dau. of Richard Ogilby. Sur. John Ogilby. p. H-4

26 June 1766. HASKINS, Edward and Martha Finney. Sur. Branch Tanner. p. H-1

26 November 1791. HASKINS, Edward and Nancy Vaughan. Sur. James Vaughan. p. H-4

20 February 1809. HASKINS, John and Sally B. Wily, dau. of John Wily. Sur. Jos: Brackett. p. H-3

26 October 1785. HASTIN, William and Amey Hastin. Wm. Hastin's consent says, "my daughter, Amey." Sur. Suton Hastin. p. H-2

10 May 1787. HASTINGS, Henry and Delila Trent. Sur. Ranson Hudgins. p. H-2

13 February 1810. HASTINGS, William and Lucy Walthall, dau. of Lucy Walthall, who consents. Wit. to consent, Thomas Worsham and Wm. Walthall. Sur. Thomas Worsham. p. H-4

16 August 1797. HASTINS, Clayton and Judith Thomson, dau. of David Thomson. Sur. Burwell Coleman. p. H-3

28 October 1806. HATCHER, Thomas and Ann H. Brackett, dau. of Ludwell Brackett, whose consent says, Ann Harris Brackett. Sur. Joseph Brackett. p. H-4

25 September 1767. HATCH"(E)"TT, Archer and Eliza King. Sur. Thos: A. Jones. p. H-1

26 January 1786. HAWKS, John and Ann Jones, who writes her own consent. Sur. Godfrey Tucker. Married 9 February by Rev. Devereux Jarratt. p. H-2

10 August 1781. HAWKS, Joshua and Pheby Wilson. Sur. John Wilson. p. H-1

29 July 1808. HAWKS, Joshua, Jr. and Lucy Allen. Sur. John B. Hawks. p. H-3

14 September 1805. HAWKINS, Grief B. and Fatha Coleman. Daniel Coleman writes: "Let Grief B. Hockins and Fatha Coleman have a license." Wit. to request, Samuel Ligon and Grief Powell. Sur. Richard Powell. p. H-3

Returned 28 August 1788. HAWKINS, Robert and Eliz^a
Smith. Married by Rev. John Pollard. Minister's Return.

8 December 1774. HAWKINS, William and Delila Martin,
dau. of George Martin, whose consent is dated 8 December,
1774. Wit. to consent, John Morris and Peter B-----.
Sur. Thomas Huddleston. p. H-1
(NOTE: The Register has 1772 - consent is 1774.)

5 March 1763. HAWKINS, Zachariah and Elizabeth Wilkerson. Sur. John Drinkard. p. H-1

12 December 1783. HAYWOOD, Randolph and Jane Asselin,
dau. of David Asselin, whose consent says Jean. Wit. to
consent, Sam Cobbs and Thos: Asselin. Sur. Thomas Asselin. p. H-2

18 April 1767. HENDERSON, James and Mary Marshall Parham
Booker. Sur. Albert M. Lubekin. p. H-1

24 May 1792. HENDERSON, James and Mary Ogilby. Sur.
Richard C. Ogilby. Married 31 May by Rev. Edmund Talley.
p. H-3
(NOTE: The report of this marriage is headed: "Little ,
Glebe, May 4, 1793", and signed: "Edmund Talley, Minister
of the Protestant Episcopal Church.").

21 December 1786. HENDRICK, Bernard and Jenny Morris,
dau. of Moses Morris, who consents. Wit. to consent,
Walter Morris and Francis Pollard. Sur. Walter Morris.
p. H-2

3 July 1798. HENDRICK, Garland and Ann Webster, dau. of
Anthony Webster. Sur. Bernard G. Hendrick. p. H-4

24 January 1785. HENDRICK, John and Sabein Garrett, of
this County. Sur. Zachariah Hendrick. p. H-2

19 July 1793. HENDRICK, John and Lucy Wright. Her
Guardian is Thos: Ligon. Sur. Richard Ligon. Married
25 July by Rev. James McGlasson. p. H-3

27 September 1787. HENDRICK, Pendleton and Elizabeth Wray,
who writes her own consent. Wit. to consent, John Hendrick and Thos: Wray. Sur. John Hendrick. Married by
Rev. John Pollard. p. H-2

23 December 1815. HENLEY, Patrick and Nancy Blankenship, who writes her own consent. Wit. to consent, Benjamin Maddox, and he testifies Nancy is of age. Sur.
Benjamin Maddox. p. H-4

10 December 1804. HICKMAN, William and Ann Eggleston.
Sur. Joseph Eggleston. p. H-3

22 September 1774. HIGHTOWER, John and Mary Edmundson,
of Nottoway Parish. Sur. George Hightower. p. H-1

2 October 1787. HIGHTOWER, Richard and Sallie Hightower,
dau. of Joshua Hightower, who consents. Wit. to consent,
Joshua Hightower, Junr. and William Hightower. Sur. Bur-
rell Featherston. p. H-2

In: "List since 1786. HIGHTOWER, William and Kate Trotter. Married by Rev. Simeon Walton. Minister's Return.

27 June 1763. HILL, James and Ann Booker, of this County.
Sur. Edmund Booker. p. H-1

28 June 1781. HILL, James and Frances Booker. Sur.
Edmond Booker. p. H-1

11 February 1802. HILLSMAN, James and Lucy Clements.
Sur. John Pride, Jr. Married 11 February by Rev. John
Skurrey. p. H-4

17 December 1792. HILLSMAN, Jesse and Elizabeth Moore,
dau. of Joseph and Susannah Moore. Sur. Blackburne
Hughes. Married by Rev. John Brunskill. p. H-3

28 October 1790. HINTON, Peter Thompson and Prudence
Scott. Sur. Peter Jones. p. H-2

In: "List since October 1788." HOBSON, Andrew and
Susannah Watson. Married by Rev. John Pollard. Minister's Return.

28 January 1777. HOBSON, William and Nancy Bracket.
Sur. Thomas **Brackett**. p. H-1

22 December 1810. HOLCOMBE, Thomas A. and Mary A.
Royall. Sur. William Royall. p. H-4

1 June 1804. HOLLOWAY, John and Sarah Tucker. Sur.
David Meredith. Married 2 June by Rev. William Dier.
p. H-3

12 September 1786. HOLLOWAY (Halloway?), William and
Margaret Jackson, who writes her own consent. Wit. to
consent, Reuben Wright. William Yates testifies she is
of age. Sur. Abraham Dumhert. p. H-2

24 October 1781. HOLMES, Isaac and Elizabeth T. Brooking. Sur. Vivion Brooking. p. H-1

20 October 1752. HOLT, David and Betty Hall, dau. of John Hall, whose consent says, "my daughter." Wit. to consent, E. Munford and D_____ Munf_____. P. H-1 (This bond is mutilated.)

2 December 1804. HOLT, David and Selina Seay, dau. of James Seay. Sur. William Wright. Married 4 December by Rev. John Pollard. p. H-3

27 September 1809. HOLT, David and Lucy Foster. Sur. Anthony Foster. p. H-3

6 November 1783. HOLT, Dudley and Sarah Jones, of this County. Sur. Thomas Jones. p. H-3

21 December 1802. HOLT, James and Sally Jones. Sur. Pleasant Wright. Married 23 December 1802 by Rev. John Pollard. p. H-4

6 May 1813. HOLT, James and Asenath Morris, dau of Sarah Morris, whose consent says her daughter is of age. Wit. to consent, Edward Farley, who is surety, and he testifies Asenath is of age. Married 6 May by Rev. John Skurrey. p. H-4

23 December 1799. HOLT, John and Sally Clardy. Sur. Richard Holt. Married 23 December by Rev. John Skurrey. p. H-3

17 January 1782. HOLT, Richard and Mary Farley. Married by Rev. Jeremiah Walker. Minister's Return.

14 February 1809. HOLT, Thomas and Any Seay, dau. of Dudley Seay. Sur. David Holt. Married 16 February by Rev. Thomas Pettus. p. H-3

26 January 1809. HOLT, William and Rebecca Jones, who writes her own consent. Wit. to consent, Paschal Mc-Glasson and Thomas Webster. Sur. Paschal McGlasson. Married 26 January by Rev. John Skurrey. p. H-4

22 February 1791. HOOD, Abraham and Sarah Tucker. Sur. Henry Tucker. Married 1 March by Rev. Robert Walthall, who says, Abraham Hood, Planter. p. H-2

25 February 1805. HOOD, Allen T. and Elce Morgan Walden, dau. of Jane Walden. Sur. David Clay. p. H-3

16 October 1791. HOOD, Claiborne and Sally Farley Willson, who writes her own consent. Wit. to consent, Jordan Hood and John S. Butler. Sur. Jordan Hood. Married 3 November by Rev. Robert Walthall. p. H-3

28 December 1799. HOOD, Edward and Phoebe Tucker. Sur.
Abram Hood. Married 2 January 1800 by Rev. Walthall
Robertson, who says Phebe. p. H-3

23 December 1811. HOOD, Henry and Martha Murray. Sur.
Frederick Jones. p. H-4

20 December 1781. HOOD, Joel and Sally Willson. Sur.
Tucker Hood. p. H-1

29 March 1787. HOOD, John and Charlotte Tucker. Sur.
Solomon Hood. p. H-2

24 July 1800. HOOD, John and Mary Hood, who writes her
own consent. Wit. to consent, William Morgan, Jr. and
Elizabeth C. Morgan. Sur. William Morgan. Married by
Rev. Walthall Robertson. p. H-3

21 May 1793. HOOD, Jordan and Sally Clay. Sur. Charles
Donaway. p. H-4

7 January 1791. HOOD, Joshua and Patty Carpenter. Sur.
Abraham Crowder. Married 8 January by Rev. Robert Walthall. p. H-2

14 December 1799. HOOD, Lewis and Catharine Claiborne,
who writes her own consent. Sur. Joseph Howell. Married 15 December by Rev. Walthall Robertson. p. H-4

1 October 1785. HOOD, Major and Frances Merriman. Sur.
Humphrey Herndon. p. H-2

16 September 1799. HOOD, Pleasant and Clarrisy Perkinson, dau. of Isham Perkinson. Sur. Joel Bevill. p. H-3

8 September 1786. HOOD, Richard and Elizabeth Willson.
John Wilson consents. Wit. to consent, Abraham Tucker
and Nathan Shepperson. Sur. Nathan Shepperson. p. H-2

16 March 1802. HOOD, Richard and Elizabeth Kidd. Sur.
Bart. Kidd. No witnesses. This bond is not in the
Register.

29 January 1778. HOOD, Solomon and Ann Green. Sur.
Abraham Green, Jr. p. H-1
(NOTE: The Register says February - bond says January.)

21 December 1790. HOOD, Thomas and Mary Tucker. Sur.
Henry Tucker. Married 22 December by Rev. Robert Walthall, who says, Thomas Hood, Planter. p. H-2

15 September 1813. HOWARD, Benjamin P. and Judith A.
Brackett, dau. of Ludwell Brackett, who consents. Wit.
to consent, Wm. F. Carter and Thos. A. Walton. Sur. Wm.
F. Carter. Married 16 September by Rev. John H. Rice.
p. H-4

15 December 1806. HOWELL, Spencer and Mary Morgan, dau.
of William Morgan. Sur. John Wilson. Married by Rev.
William Dier. p. H-4

14 October 1795. HOWLETT, James and Lucy Mann, dau. of
Cain Mann, who consents. Wit. to consent, John Ford
Wm. Mann and Joel Mann. Sur. William Mann. p. H-3

15 February 1769. HOWLETT, William and Martha Chappell,
dau. of James Chappell, who consents. Wit. to consent,
Gulielman Howlett. Sur. Joshua Neal. p. H-1

2 May 1782. HUBBARD, Benjamin and Elizabeth Foster.
Married by Rev. Jeremiah Walker. Minister's Return.

28 August 1788. HUBBARD, James and Elizabeth Richardson,
dau. of Ruler Richardson, who consents. Wit. to consent,
David Richardson, Benjamin Borum and James Robertson.
Sur. Edmund Borum. Married by Rev. Charles Anderson.
p. H-2

12 April 1774. HUDDLESTON, Thomas and Milly Tanner,
both of Raleigh Parish. Sur. Jeremiah Tanner. p. H-1

10 August 1799. HUDDLESTON, Thomas and Patsy W. Tanner,
dau. of Robert Tanner. Sur. Wiley Huddleston. p. H-4

28 October 1779. HUDSON, Burton and Elizabeth Booker,
dau. of George Booker of this county, who consents and
is surety. p. H-1

16 September 1786. HUDSON, Daniel and Leah Dyson, who
writes her own consent. Wit. to consent, Richard Ward.
Sur. James Sturdavant. p. H-2

23 June 1785. HUDSON, James and Prudence Bruice. Sur.
Alexander Bruice. p. H-2

27 January 1777. HUDSON, Robert and Jean Booker, both
of Raleigh Parish. Sur. John Catlin Cobbs. p. H-1

18 August 1761. HUDSON, Ward and Martha Hudson, spinster. Sur. James Hudson. p. H-1

25 May 1756. HUDSON, William and Dianah Moss. Consent of
Thomas Lorton, who says: "She is orphan of Francis Moss,
late of York County, deceased, and I being her Guardian----"
Wit. to consent, Josiah Thomson and Rebeckah Bentley.
Sur. Andrew Lester, of Amelia. William Hudson is of Cum-
berland County. p. H-1

26 May 1791. HUDSON, William C. and Hannah Scott, who
writes her own consent as Hannah W. Scott on 26 May 1791.
Sur. Francis Anderson. Married by Rev. John Brunskill,
who says William Chamberlain Hudson. p. H-3

22 December 1791. HUGHES, Blackburn and Judith Booker.
Sur. John Morris. Married by Rev. John Brunskill. p. H-4

28 September 1785. HUNDLEY, Anthony and Charlotte Walton, dau. of Sherd Walton, who consents. Wit. to consent, John Mitchell, who is surety. Married by Rev.
Simeon Walton. p. H-2

26 November 1778. HUNDLEY, Josiah and Eliza Motley.
Sur. Philip Williams, Jr. p. H-1

1 February 1803. HUNDLEY, Josiah and Elizabeth Ogilby.
Sur. Richard Ogilby. Married 3 February by Rev. John
Skurrey. p. H-4

21 October 1811. HUNDLEY, William and Martha Mann, dau.
of William Mann, who consents. Wit. to consent, Archer
Mann and Thos: Hundley. Sur. Archibald Mann. Married
22 December by Rev. Thomas Pettus. p. H-4

25 May 1789. HURT, Anson and Winnefred Dunnavant, dau.
of Hodges Dunnavant, who consents. Wit. to consent,
Philip Dunnavant and Ann Dunnavant. Sur. Philip Dunnavant. Anson is son of William Hurt, who consents for
Anson "to Act for himself." p. H-2

14 February 1795. HURT, James and Nancy Allen. Sur.
David Allen. p. H-3

13 April 1795. HURT, John and Nancy Newman, dau. of
Rice Newman. Sur. Ward Furguson. p. H-4

8 January 1808. HURT, John and Elizabeth Allen. Sur.
Samuel Allen, Sr. Married 9 January by Rev. John Skurrey. p. H-4

13 November 1782. HUTCHESON, James and Anna Whitworth.
Sur. William Southall. James is son of Charles Hutche-
son, who consents. Wit. to consent, David Weatherford,
Mary Weatherford and _____ Whitlock. p. H-2

In: "List since October 1788. HUTCHESON, John and Magdalene Wadil. Married by Rev. John Pollard. Minister's Return.

31 December 1793. HUTCHESON, William and Mary Stewart, who writes her own consent. Wit. to consent, Edward Scott and John Rogers. Sur. William Booker. Married 4 January 1794 by Rev. John Skurrey. p. H-3

13 February 1805. HYDE, Richard and Elizabeth Sophia Roberts, who writes her own consent. Wit. to consent, Philip Roberts. Sur. Wiley Roberts. p. H-3

25 January 1782. IRBY, Charles and Martha Epes, sister of Freeman Epes, who consents for her. Sur. Chas. Erskine. p. I-1

13 December 1783. IRBY, Charles and Mary Williams, dau. of Thomas Williams, who consents. Wit. to consent, William Williams. Sur. Joseph Greenhill. p. I-1

29 October 1759. IRBY, Edwin and Mary Morgan, dau. of Sam'l. Morgan, who consents. Wit. to consent, John Mann and Elizabeth Morgan. Sur. John Mann. Edwin Irby is of Chesterfield County. p. I-1

29 January 1757. IRBY, John and Susanna Wynn. Sur. John Wynn. p. I-1

7 February 1778. IRBY, John and Jane Crenshaw, dau. of William Crenshaw, Sr., who consents. Wit. to consent, William Crenshaw and James Crenshaw. Sur. William Crenshaw. p. I-1

16 May 1782. IRBY, William and Jean Evans. Sur. John Irby. p. I-1

23 January 1781. JACKSON, Arthur and Mary Jackson. Sur. John Jackson. p. J-1

25 April 1785. JACKSON, Benedict and Molly E. Jackson. Sur. Edward Jackson. p. J-2

11 November 1776. JACKSON, Benjamin and Elizabeth Thompson, who writes her own consent, dated 10 November 1776. Both are of Raleigh Parish. Sur. John Hatchett. p. J-1

26 October 1787. JACKSON, Burwell and Lucy Farguson, dau. of Peleg Farguson, who consents. Wit. to consent, James Townes, Jr. and Benja. Ward. Sur. John Westbrook. p. J-3
(NOTE: 16 October is on outside of bond - 26 October is on inside of bond.)

9 March 1807. JACKSON, Coleman and Elizabeth Harper.
Thompson Scott, Sen., her Guardian, consents. Sur. Floid
Robertson. p. J-3

27 August 1787. JACKSON, Curtis and Sarah Bedel. Sur.
John Bedel. p. J-2

31 July 1801. JACKSON, Davis and Sally Harris, who
writes her own consent. Sur. Tarlton Cox. Married 6
August by Rev. John Pollard. p. J-3

10 February 1778. JACKSON, Francis and Martha Maddra.
Sur. Micajah Maddra. Benj: Lockett and Simon Clements,
Guardians of Francis Jackson, consent. p. J-1

24 December 1764. JACKSON, Joel and Mary Thompson, dau.
of Peter Thompson, who consents. Wit. to consent, William Hatchett, who is surety. p. J-1

28 November 1787. JACKSON, Joel and Elizabeth Jackson,
dau. of Francis Jackson, who consents. Wit. to consent,
Francis Jackson, Jr. and Billy Jackson. Sur. Francis
Jackson, Jr. Married by Rev. John Brunskill. p. J-3

19 December 1806. JACKSON, Joseph and Elizabeth Cardwell, dau. of Richd Cardwell. Sur. George Cardwell.
p. J-3

8 November 1784. JACKSON, Moses and Frances Fields, who
writes her own consent. Wit. to consent, Mary Booker
and Ben Overstreet. Sur. Hodges Dunnavant. p. J-2

8 October 1803. JACKSON, Moses and Rhoda Dunnavant.
Sur. John Crittington. Married 9 October by Rev. William Dier. p. J-3

22 October 1767. JACKSON, William and Phebe Seay, dau.
of Jacob Seay, who consents. Wit. to consent, Francis
Seay and Edmund Borum. Sur. Edmund Borum. Matthew Jackson consents for son, Tom William Jackson. p. J-1

25 December 1799. JACKSON, Wily and Betsy Seay, dau. of
James Seay. Sur. Marshall Seay. Married 26 December by
Rev. John Skurrey. p. J-4

10 January 1788. JAMES, Jesse and Polly Thomas, dau. of
Edmund Thomas, who consents. Wit. to consent, William
Cryer and Robt. Booth. Sur. Law^s Hobbs. p. J-3

24 September 1778. JAMES, John and Ann Clemment. Sur.
Edward Tabb. p. J-1

23 November 1786. JAMES, John and Hannah Pollard, dau.
of Joseph Pollard, who consents. Wit. to consent, _____
Pollard and James McGlasson. Sur. James McGlasson. John
is son of John James, who consents. p. J-2

28 February 1760. JAMES, Thomas and Martha Butler,
widow. Sur. William Booker. p. J-1

30 January 1784. JEFFERIS, Thomas, Jr. and Elizabeth
Fowlkes, dau. of Jennings Fowlkes, whose consent says
Thomas Jeffress. Wit. to consent, John Fowlkes and Henry
Fowlkes. Sur. John Fowlkes. p. J-2

18 November 1801. JEFFERSON, Daniel and Polly Bevill.
Sur. Claiborne Bevill. p. J-3

30 April 1800. JEFFERSON, John G. and Ann Booker. Sur.
James Townes, Jr. Married 1 May by Rev. David Thomson.
p. J-4

27 March 1788. JEFFRESS, Coleman and Mary Fowlkes.
Sur. Jennings Fowlkes. Married by Rev. S. Walton.
p. J-3

14 December 1764. JENKINS, James and Rebecca Overton.
Sur. James Hill. p. J-1

24 March 1768. JENNINGS, Dickerson and Frances Bagley,
dau. of George Bagley, who consents. Wit. to consent,
George Bagley, Junr. and James Bagley. Sur. George
Bagley, Junr. William Jennings consents for son, Dicker-
son. Wit. to his consent, James Anderson and Charles
Anderson. p. J-1

1 October 1785. JENNINGS, Joseph and Mary Jeffries.
Thos: Jeffries consents. Sur. John Fowlkes. p. J-2

31 August 1784. JENNINGS, Moody and Ann Hundley. Joel
Hundley, Ann's Guardian, consents. Wit. to consent, B.
Caffery. Sur. John Jennings. p. J-2

25 October 1780. JENNINGS, Peter and Celia Moore, dau.
of John Moore, who consents. Wit. to consent, Robert
Jennings and John Drewry. This is consent only, and
NOT in the Register.

12 December 1786. JENNINGS, William and W. Fanny Jones,
dau. of William Jones, who consents. Wit. to consent,
John Mitchell and James Mitchell. Sur. John Jones.
p. J-2

20 September 1786. JESSE, Thomas and Sarah James, who writes her own consent. Wit. to consent, Wm. Mosby. Sur. Paulin Anderson. Thomas Jesse is of Powhatan County. p. J-2

11 January 1785. JETER, Allen and Judith Crowder, dau. of Wil: Crowder, who consents. Sur. Francis Anderson. p. J-2

23 January 1760. JETER, Ambrose and Jean Stern, spinster, dau. of Ann Stern, whose consent "as mother and Guardian of Jean," says Ambrose Jeter is of Caroline County. Wit. to consent, John Jeter and Elizabeth Stern. Sur. John Jeter. p. J-1

29 September 1779. JETER, Ambrose and Mary Farley, widow, of this County. Sur. Thomas Hall. p. J-1

18 May 1756. JETER, James and Percilla Yarbugh, who signs her own consent: **Persilla Yarbrough.** Alex Erskine and John Winn and John Hall testify they believe Persilla of age. Sur. John Jeter. p. J-1

31 December 1794. JETER, John and Jinney Chaffin, dau. of Joshua Chaffin. Sur. John Chaffin. p. J-4

27 April 1801. JETER, John and Ann Scott. George Scott consents. Sur. Thompson Scott. Married 28 April by Rev. John Skurrey. p. J-3
(NOTE: Register says 1 April - bond says 27 April.)

23 October 1783. JETER, Presley and Phebe Carter. Sur. Richard Ligon. p. J-2

11 July 1785. JETER, Reuben and Martha Marshall, "alias Crowder." Consent of William Crowder, her father-in-law, says: "Martha Marshall, alias Crowder, is of full age." Wit. to consent, John Crowder. Sur. Ambrose Jeter. p. J-2

15 October 1785. JETER, Rodophil and Lucy Gills, dau. of John Gills, Sr., who consents. Wit. to consent, Anthony Crenshaw and Sam Gills. Sur. Anthony Crenshaw. p. J-2

9 June 1801. JETER, Tilman E. and Sally W. Hannah. Sur. Anthony Webster, Junr. Richard Broaddus, of Richmond, Tilman's Guardian, consents and says he is under age. Wit. to consent, Joshua Chaffin and David Chaffin. p. J-3

26 November 1807. JOHNS, John A. and Elizabeth Ann Morgan. Sur. John Morgan. p. J-3

2 February 1804. JOHNSON, Allen and Philadelphia Jones. Sur. Matthew Booth. p. J-3

28 July 1796. JOHNSON, James and Mary Gibbs. Sur. Peter Webster. p. J-3

24 March 1784. JOHNSON, Philip and Phebe Clay, both of this County. Sur. John Clay. p. J-2

24 January 1793. JOHNSON, Thomas and Lucy Crowder. Sur. William Crowder. Married by Rev. John Skurrey. p. J-3

In: List since October 1787. JOHNSON, William and Susanna Bryan. Married by Rev. S. Walton. Minister's Return.

12 December 1792. JOHNSON, William and Polly Askew (Haskew?), who writes her own consent and says she is an orphan. John Watkins requests this license. Sur. Benjamin Pollard. Married 20 December by Rev. John Watkins. p. J-3

10 September 1812. JOHNSON, Wilson and Polly Wright, who writes her own consent. Wit. to consent, Richard Ligon and Pleasant Wright. Sur. Pleasant Wright, who testifies Polly is of age. Married 25 November by Rev. John Pollard. p. J-4

20 October 1796. JOLLY, Henry and Sarah Hurt. Sur. Cary Hurt. p. J-3

29 September 1800. JOLLY, Henry and Betsy Bell. Sur. John Bell. Married 2 October by Rev. John Skurrey. p. J-3

21 April 1802. JOLLY, Henry and Elizabeth W. Fagg, dau. of John Fagg. Sur. John M. Smithey. Married 22 April by Rev. John Pollard. p. J-4

24 December 1783. JONES, Abraham and Lucy Atkinson Jackson, dau. of Isaac Jackson, who consents. Sur. Benjamin Lawson. p. J-2

17 April 1782. JONES, Adam and Nancy Har--son, dau. of Richard Harrison of Nottoway Parish, who consents. Wit. to consent, Wm. Barksdale and John Elliott. Sur. William Maynard. p. J-2   (Bond is mutilated.)

17 December 1810. JONES, Anderson H. and Nancy W. Seay, who writes her own consent. Edward Claybrook testifies Nancy is "upwards of 21." Sur. Edward Claybrook. p. J-4

28 November 1793. JONES, Archer and Frances Branch Scott, dau. of James Scott. Sur. Richard Archer. p. J-4

11 February 1777. JONES, Batt and Margaret Ward, dau. of Rowland Ward, Senr., who consents. Wit. to consent, Richard Jones and Rowland Ward, Junr. Sur. Rowland Ward, Junr. p. J-1

18 December 1802. JONES, Branch and Dorotha Anderson. Sur. Claiborne Anderson. p. J-3

25 September 1800. JONES, Cadwallader and Dorothey F. Featherston, dau. of Charles Featherston. Sur. Richard Jones, Jr. p. J-4

23 September 1762. JONES, Charles and Ann Towns. Sur. Robert Jones. p. J-1

28 October 1784. JONES, Charles and Hester Mayo Jones, who writes her own consent. Wit. to consent, William Worsham and Robert Jones. Sur. Robert Jones. p. J-2

4 September 1784. JONES, Daniel and Catherine Ward, who writes her own consent. Wit. to consent, Wm. Hayes, who is Surety. p. J-2

28 November 1800. JONES, David C. and Rebecca W. Jones, dau. of Robt. Jones, who consents. Sur. Chamberlain Jones. p. J-3

2 December 1776. JONES, Edward and Martha Jones. Both are of Raleigh Parish. Sur. Thomas Jones. p. J-1

9 October 1787. JONES, Edward and Elizabeth Jones. Sur. Peter Robertson. p. J-2

2 May 1795. JONES, Edward and Prudence Jones, dau. of Robert Jones, who consents. Sur. John Roberts and Thomas Jones. p. J-3

10 August 1812. JONES, Edward H. and Elizabeth T. Bott, dau. of Lucy Bott, who consents. Wit. to consent, Mary Randolph and James Bott. Sur. Lucy Bott. p. J-4

26 January 1792. JONES, Elijah and Lucy Ligon. Sur. Thos: Ligon. Married 29 January by Rev. Abner Watkins. p. J-3

23 October 1801. JONES, Elisha and Nancy Holt. Sur. James Holt. Married 25/28 October by Rev. John Pollard. (Two lists.) p. J-3

5 September 1756. JONES, Francis and Rebecca Green, who writes her own consent and signs her name Rebekah. Wit. to consent, Martha Green and John Wills. Sur. Abraham Green. p. J-1

27 December 1787. JONES, Frederick and Catharine Anderson, dau. of Henry Anderson, who is surety. Married 10 January 1788 by Rev. John Brunskill. p. J-2

24 April 1800. JONES, Frederick and Frances A. Vaughan, who writes her own consent. Sur. Ben Overstreet. p. J-3

5 October 1781. JONES, Harrison and Ann Ligon, dau. of Wm. Ligon. Sur. John Hughes, Jr. p. J-2

24 September 1792. JONES, Henry Winn and Ann C. Ellington, dau. of David Ellington, whose consent says: "my daughter, Anna C. Ellington." Wit. to consent, William Farley, who is surety. p. J-3
(NOTE: Bond says Ann - her father says Anna.)

30 March 1761. JONES, John and Martha Redford, who writes her own consent. Sur. Thomas Lowry. p. J-1

31 January 1769. JONES, John, Jr. and Elizabeth Crawley, dau. of William Crawley, Gent., of Amelia, who consents. Wit. to consent, Ben Ward and Thos: Jones. Sur. Thos. Jones. John Jones, Jr. is of Dinwiddie County. p. J-1

29 November 1783. JONES, John and Sarah Turner, of this County. Sur. David Wallace. p. J-2

27 September 1796. JONES, Lew and Prudence Ward. Rowland Ward, her Guardian, consents that "Lew Jones marry Miss Prudence Ward, orphan of Rowland Ward, deceased." Wit. to consent, Robert Jones and Richd H. Jones. Sur. Peter Jones. p. J-4   (Lewelling Jones?)

13 December 1763. JONES, Nelson and Lettice Greenhill. Sur. David Greenhill. p. J-1

7 January 1801. JONES, Nelson and Martha Cousins, dau. of William Cousins, who consents. Wit. to consent, Robert Cousins and John Wilson. Sur. Robert Cousins. Married 15 January by Rev. Charles Roper "by ceremonies of the Methodist Episcopal Church." p. J-3

20 February 1746. JONES, Peter and Sarah Tanner. Sur. Clement Read. Wit. to bond, Wm. Wilkins, Junr. p. J-1

16 February 1759. JONES, Peter and Martha Jones, dau. of Richard Jones, who consents. Wit. to consent, Henry Jones, who is surety. p. J-1

12 April 1775. JONES, Peter and Elizabeth Wilkerson, both of Raleigh Parish. Sur. John Jones. p. J-1

27 July 1791. JONES, Peter and Catherine Chappell. Sur. Alex^r Jones. p. J-3

28 November 1769. JONES, Richard, Junr. and Mary Robertson, dau. of James Robertson, deceased, "late of Chesterfield County." John Winn, Mary's Guardian consents. Consent dated 6 November 1769. Wit. to consent, Thomas Boring and Abram Smith. Sur. William Gooch. Richard is son of Richard Jones, Senr., whose consent is dated 25 November 1769. p. J-1

15 November 1774. JONES, Richard and Martha Ward, dau. of Rowland Ward, Senr., who consents. Wit. to consent, Thomas Jones and Rowland Ward, Junr. Sur. Rowland Ward, Junr. p. J-1
(NOTE: This marriage has been reported differently. The above was checked with the original bond and the original consent. K.B.W.)

15 June 1796. JONES, Richard and Frances Jones. Sur. Peter Jones. p. J-4

16 June 1750. JONES, Robert and Sarah Scott, "relict of Joseph Scott, deceased." Sur. Thos. Nash. Robert Jones is of Lunenburg County. p. J-1

5 June 1783. JONES, Robert and Ann Ward, dau. of Rowland Ward. Sur. Edward Jones. p. J-2

27 April 1786. JONES, Robert and Mary Gooch. Sur. John Gooch. p. J-2

11 May 1782. JONES, Samuel and Mary Giles, dau. of William Giles, who consents. Sur. Robert Jones. p. J-2

24 November 1785. JONES, Samuel and Delphe Farguson, dau. of Peleg Farguson, who consents. Sur. John Farguson. Married 12 December by Rev. Devereux Jarratt. p. J-2

6 February 1790. JONES, Samuel and Patsy Eans, dau. of Josiah Eans, whose consent says, "my daughter, Patsy." Sur. John Sudbury. p. J-3

12 October 1809. JONES, Spottswood and Susanna I. Branch. On the bond: "Her father present and gave consent but his name not given." Sur. Mathew Branch, Junr. Married 12 October by Rev. John Pollard, Senr. p. J-4

20 July 1763. JONES, Thomas and Sarah Jones, of
Raleigh Parish. Sur. Daniel Jones. p. J-1

28 October 1784. JONES, Thomas and Prudence Jones. Sur.
Edward Jones. This bond is not in the Register.

23 July 1787. JONES, Thomas and Dorothy Jones. Sur.
Peter Branch. p. J-2

6 March 1756. JONES, William and Lettis Hightower,
spinster. Robert Kennon consents. Consent dated 4
March 1756. Wit. to consent, John Rogers and John
Jackson. Sur. Thomas Claiborne. p. J-1

22 October 1784. JONES, William and Mary Ham. Sur.
Frederick Dunnavant. p. J-2

9 November 1763. JONES, Wood and Amy Watson, widow, of
Nottoway Parish, who writes her own consent. Sur.
Andrew Redford. p. J-1

18 August 1800. JONES, Wood, Sr. and Martha Jones.
J. Townes testifies she "is of full age." Sur. Peter
Jones, Jr. p. J-4

6 February 1781. JORDAN, Freeman and Ann Cocke, dau. of
Peter Cocke, who consents. Wit. to consent, John Locke
and John Jordan. Sur. Samuel Jordan. p. J-2

15 March 1796. KERR, John and Molley Claybrook. Sur.
Peter Claybrook. Married 16 March by Rev. James McGlasson. p. K-1

30 July 1801. KIBBLE, Walter and Sally R. Hudson. Her
Guardian, Richeson Booker writes:
"To Ja. Townes, Clerk of Amelia,
                                  Sir, you are at liberty,
if you think proper, to grant a license to Mr. W. Kibble
and Miss Sally R. Hudson." Signed: "R. Booker
                                  Petersburg, July 3, 1801."
Sur. Samuel Ford. p. K-1

24 May 1806. KIDD, Bartholomew and Polly Moore. Sur.
Joseph Hillsman. Married 24 May by Rev. Zachariah G.
Leigh. p. K-1

12 June 1786. KIDD, George and Mary Southall, dau. of
James Southall, who consents. Wit. to consent, George
Southall and Dan¹ Southall. Sur. Jesse Coleman. p. K-1

13 November 1810. KIDD, Jasper and Fanny Thompson, dau.
of Thomas Thompson, who consents. Wit. to consent, Isaac
Pollard and W, T. Craddock. Sur. Thos. Thompson. p. K-1

26 December 1759. KING, John and Mary Powell, dau. of
Joseph Powell, who is surety. p. K-1

14 December 1787. KNIGHT, Coleman and Nancy Knight, dau.
of Peter Knight, who consents. Wit. to consent, Rich^d
Mays and Peter Robertson. Sur. John Harrison. Married
by Rev. Charles Anderson. p. K-1

28 November 1759. LACY, Theophilus and Martha Cocke,
spinster, dau. of Abraham Cocke, who consents. Sur.
Richard Ellis. Theophilus Lacy is of Halifax County.
p. L-1

12 March 1789. LAND, William and Susanna Bennett, dau.
of John Bennett, who consents. Wit. to consent, Briton
Moore and Anderson Moore. Sur. Richard Bennett. Married by Rev. John Finney. p. S-2
(NOTE: The Register has William Sands - the bond, consent and Minister's Return have William Land.)

4 February 1768. LANE, John and Sarah Reams, who writes
her own consent. Sur. Frederick Reams. John Lane is of
Goochland County. p. L-1

2 October 1783. LAWSON, Benjamin and Ellen Worsham.
Sur. Zachariah Leigh. p. L-1

23 November 1769. LEA, Andrew and Elizabeth Dudley, dau.
of Thomas Dudley, who consents. Wit. to consent, William
Dudley and Jane Sneed. Sur. Thomas Dudley, Jr. p. L-1

7 December 1782. LEAGUE, Benjamin and Anne Hubbard.
Sur. Edmund League. Wit. to bond, Thos. Mumford, W. T.
Moulson and John Wily, D. C. p. L-1

1 April 1793. LEAGUE, Edmund and Mary Beadle, dau. of
John Beadle. Sur. William Foster. p. L-1

25 May 1809. LEAGUE, Joel and Mary Holt. Sur. Allen
Jeter. Married 28 May by Rev. John Pollard. p. L-2

1 February 1797. LEATH, Jesse and Harriet Marshall, dau.
of Robert Marshall. Sur. Robert Marshall, Jr. p. L-1

3 February 1796. LEATH, Lewis and Clarissa Walthall,
dau. of William Walthall, Sr. Sur. John Clemons. p. L-2

21 November 1757. LEIGH, John and Elizabeth Greenhill,
spinster, dau. of David Greenhill, who consents. Wit.
to consent, Sarah Anderson and Paschal Greenhill. Sur.
Benjamin Ward. p. L-1

15 October 1800. LEIGH, John T. and Elizabeth F. Townes.
Sur. John L. Townes. Married 16 October by Rev. John
Skurrey. p. L-1

24 September 1813. LEIGH, John T. and Rebecca W. Giles.
Sur. Thomas W. Powell. Married 24 September by Rev.
John Skurrey. p. L-2

17 December 1815. LEIGH, John T. and Cary J. Clay.
Jesse Clay consents. Wit. to consent, A. T. Clay.
On December 17th Daniel Clay testifies he saw Jesse Clay
consent. This is consent only.

28 September 1811. LEIGH, William and Ann L. Townes.
Sur. Zachariah Leigh. p. L-2

5 January 1784. LEIGH, Zachariah G. and Priscilla Allen
Townes, dau. of John Townes, Sr., whose consent says
Zachariah Greenhill Leigh. Sur. Benjamin Lawson. p. L-1

2 June 1759. LeNeve, John and Susanna Dawson, dau. of
I (?) Dawson, who consents. Wit. to consent, John Gra-
ham. Sur. William Booker. p. L-1

7 December 1784. LEONARD, Frederick and Polly Tucker.
Sur. Randolph Simmons. p. L-1

8 August 1792. LESTER, Archer and Dicey Coleman. Sur.
John Green. Married 12 August by Rev. Robert Walthall,
who says Archer Lester, Planter. p. L-1

18 February 1812. LESTER, Archibald and Sally Graves,
who writes her own consent. Wit. to consent, John
Hardy and Delphy Johnson. Sur. John Hardy. Married 20
February by Rev. James Chappell. p. L-2

23 October 1788. LESTER, Claiborne and _____ Reams.
Sur. John Perkinson. p. L-1   (Bond mutilated.)

12 November 1789. LESTER, Riland and Rebecah Powell,
dau. of Robert Powell, who consents. Wit. to consent,
Abraham Powell and John Powell. Sur. John Powell.
Married by Rev. John Brunskill. p. L-1

In: List since October 1787. LETT, Nance and Caty
Philips. Married by Rev. Simeon Walton. Minister's
Return.

5 December 1804. LEWELLING, Moses and Sally Grant.
Sur. William Tanner. p. L-1

XVII January 1758. LEWIS, Henry and Elizabeth Ford.
Sur. Thos: Claiborne. p. L-1

14 August 1781. LEWIS, John and Joanna Lipscomb. Permission of G. Lenore (?), dated 13 August, 1781 says, "I am Guardian of the young lady." Sur. Isham Malone. p. L-1

24 January 1784. LEWIS, William and Judith Archer Hardaway. Sur. John Royall, Jr. p. L-1

28 March 1765. LIGON, Richard and Mary Bagley, dau. of George Bagley, who consents and he is surety. p. L-1

28 April 1808. LIGON, Richard W. and Nancy C. Smithey, dau. of Joshua Smithey. Sur. Robert L. Smithey. Married "the last day of May" by Rev. John Pollard. p. L-2

3 June 1769. LIGON, Robert and Sarah Cary Mitchell, dau. of James Mitchell, who consents. Wit. to consent, John Dolly and Anderson Mitchell. Sur. John Mitchell. p. L-1

11 November 1809. LIGON, Samuel and Lucy H. Drake, dau. of William Drake. Sur. John Southall. p. L-1

26 January 1802. LIGON, Thomas and Betsy Beacham, dau. of Prudence Beacham. Sur. Anderson Stone. Married by Rev. John Pollard. p. L-2

20 October 1803. LINCH, John and Susannah Allen, dau. of Samuel Allen. Sur. Samuel Allen, Jr. Married 24 October by Rev. John Skurrey. p. L-2

2 June 1788. LESAIN, David and Sally Dunnavant, who writes her own consent as **Salle** to David **Le Sain**. Sur. Anselm Bailey. p. L-1

18 June 1784. LOCKETT, Abraham and Sarah Hill, who writes her own consent. Wit. to consent, William Ford. Sur. William Ford, Sr. p. L-1

1 November 1797. LOCKETT, Benjamin and Mary Ann League, who writes her own consent. Wit. to consent, Peter Farley and John Lockett. Sur. John Lockett. p. L-1

22 October 1798. LOCKETT, Jacob and Mary League, who writes her own consent. Sur. William Holt. Married 25 October by Rev. John Skurrey. p. L-1

30 April 1804. LOCKETT, Jacob and Mason Crenshaw, whose Guardian, Benjamin Dowdy, is surety. p. L-2

3 June 1745. LORTON, Thomas and Elizabeth Moss, widow. Sur. Norvell Baskervyle. p. L-1

23 May 1806. LUMPKIN, Anthony and Eliza Waugh. Sur.
Tom F. Willson. p. L-2

6 November 1787. LUMPKIN, Moses and Sarah Leonard.
Sur. Frederick Leonard. Married by Rev. John Brunskill. p. L-1

18 December 1815. LUNCEFORD, James and Elizabeth Brewer,
who writes her own consent to James Lunceford. Sur.
Isham Belcher. p. L-2

22 November 1796. McCOY, Nathan and Sally Worsham.
Sur. David Worsham. p. M-4

26 February 1787. McDEARMAN, Michael and Sally Ford.
Garret Ford requests this license and says Sally is of
age. Sur. Henry Ford. p. M-2

14 March 1789. McDEARMAN, Richard and Lette Ford. Sur.
Albery Ford. Married by Rev. John Finney. p. M-3

2 December 1788. McGLASSON, James and Mildred Crenshaw,
who writes her own consent. Sur. Andrew Christian.
Married by Rev. John Finney. p. M-2

18 August 1804. McGLASSON, Paschal and Phebe W. Webster. Sur. John Webster, Junr. p. M-3

11 November 1796. McGLASSON, William and Polly Wright,
dau. of Martha Raggles. Sur. John Hendrick. p. M-5

29 November 1803. McKAY, William and Elizabeth Morris,
dau. of Redosha Morris. Sur. Rodophil Jeter. Married
by Rev. John Pollard. p. M-4

13 May 1802. McNAMAR, John and Sally S. Asselin. Sur.
Joseph Foster. Married 15 May by Rev. John Pollard.
p. M-4   (Is this McNamarr?)

24 October 1759. McNUTT, James and Joan Wallace, who
writes her own consent, dated 24 October 1759. Charles
Irby certifies she is of age on the same date. Sur.
John Wallace. p. M-1

24 October 1813. MABEN, David, Jr. and Ann E. T. Perkinson, dau. of Thos. Perkinson, who consents. Wit. to
consent, J. T. Rison and W. E. Noble. Sur. Peter Rison.
Married 25 October by Rev. John Skurrey. p. M-5

-- January 1810. MABEN, Mathew and Martha C. Perkinson.
Sur. Peter Rison. Wit. to bond, John Gordon. p. M-5

12 June 1809. MADDEIRA, Geo. Washington Davis and Elizabeth Sharp Woodward. Sur. Thomas Woodward. p. M-4
(Madeira or Madenna?)

28 August 1800. MADDEIRA, John T. and Patty Avery, who writes her own consent. Wit. to consent, Joel Avary and George Avary. Sur. George Avary. p. M-4

16 June 1814. MAJORS, Samuel H. and Catharine P. Webster, who writes her own consent. Wit. to consent, William W. Hall, who is surety. Married 18 June by Rev. James Chappell. p. M-5

10 September 1778. MALLORY, Francis and Frances Allen. Sur. Francis White. p. M-1

4 February 1769. MALONE, Isham and Elizabeth Hamlin, dau. of William Hamlin, who consents. Sur. James Bagley. p. M-1

29 July 1762. MALONE, Robert and Elizabeth Bridgforth. Sur. Alex^r Bruce. p. M-1

6 March 1783. MANN, Abel and Keziah Roach. Sur. Joseph Roach. p. M-2

25 February 1796. MANN, Abner and Mary Newby, Sur. Jesse Newby. p. M-4

17 September 1806. MANN, Archibald and Polly Berry. Sur. John Berry. p. M-3

1 December 1791. MANN, Cain and Mary Ford, who writes her own consent and says Cain Mann, Senr. Sur. John Finney. p. M-4

24 September 1795. MANN, Cain and Prinsey Belcher. Sur. Robert Mann. p. M-3

9 June 1800. MANN, David and Mary Old. Sur. Abner Chappell. p. M-3
(NOTE: The Register says Winney - the bond says Mary.)

22 December 1806. MANN, David and Lucy Hawks. Sur. Daniel Mann. p. M-3

23 November 1815. MANN, George F. and Elizabeth Ford. Sur. Daniel Mann. Married 25 November by Rev. James Chappell. p. M-5

27 February 1784. MANN, James and Sally Cheatham, of Amelia County. Sur. John Green. p. M-2

27 December 1792. MANN, Joel and Frances Wilson, dau. of William Wilson. Sur. John Mann. Married 29 December by Rev. Robert Walthall, who says Joel Mann, Planter. p. M-3

21 December 1798. MANN, Joel and Eliza Wills. Sur. John Cousins. p. M-3

14 May 1759. MANN, John and Sarah Ford, who writes her own consent. (No witnesses.) John Wright, her Guardian, consents. Wit. to consent, John Right and Mary Right. Sur. Henry Anderson. p. M-1

18 April 1785. MANN, John and Sarah Hayes. Richard Hayes consents. Wit. to consent, Jno. Finney. Sur. Thomas Old. p. M-2

20 June 1805. MANN, John and Elizabeth B. Brooking, dau. of William Brooking, who consents. Sur. Robert E. Brooking. p. M-3

29 February 1811. MANN, Levi and Polley Bowman, who writes her own consent. Wit. to consent, Wm. Keeling and Mary Farley. Archer Mann testifies she is of age. Sur. Peter Farley. p. M-5

25 May 1815. MANN, Pleasant H. and Martha H. Green, who writes her own consent. Wit. to consent, J. Quarles and John Bottom. Elizabeth Green testifies Martha is of age. Sur. Peter Burton. Married 28 May by Rev. James Chappell. p. M-5

8 January 1799. MANN, Samuel and Nancy Perkinson. Isham Perkinson consents. Sur. John Reams. p. M-3

30 December 1787. MANN, William and Mary Hundley. Consent of Richard Hundley. Wit. to consent, John Angell and John Hundley. Sur. John Hundley. Married by Rev. Charles Anderson. p. M-2

4 September 1745. MARR, Gideon and Sarah Miller. Sur. John Woodson. p. M-1

1 January 1783. MARSHAL, Abraham and Elizabeth Osborne. Sur. Joseph Osborne. p. M-2

22 June 1768. MARSHALL, Alexander and Ann Walthall. Sur. Charles Walthall. p. M-1

23 December 1783. MARSHALL, Daniel and Elizabeth Marshall. Elizabeth Marshall consents. Sur. Peter Ellington. p. M-1

13 December 1786. MARSHALL, Daniel and Sarah Thompson, dau. of Morgan Thompson, whose consent says Sally. Wit. to consent, Joseph Wills and Wm. Worsham. Sur. Joseph Wills. Married by Rev. John Brunskill. p. M-2

18 November 1782. MARSHALL, John and Betsy Walthall, dau. of William Walthall, who consents. Wit. to consent, Henry Walthall and Daniel Hardaway. Sur. Henry Walthall. p. M-2

6 December 1815. MARSHALL, Warren and Nancy Marshall, who writes her own consent. Wit. to consent, William Marshall and John Marshall, who testify Nancy is of age. Sur. William Marshall. Married 8 December by Rev. James Chappell. p. M-5

19 February 1765. MARSHALL, William, Senr. and Judith Willis. Sur. Rolfe Eldridge. p. M-1

7 November 1805. MARTIN, Jesse and Kitty Rucker. Sur. Joshua Rucker. Married 7 November by Rev. John Skurrey. p. M-4

12 April 1804. MARTIN, John and Sally Rucker. Joshua Rucker consents. Wit. to consent, Pleasant Rucker and Benjamin Martin. Sur. Pleasant Rucker. Married 12 April by Rev. John Skurrey. p. M-4

24 December 1782. MARTIN, Reuben and Nancy Crittington, dau. of Henry Crittington, who consents. Wit. to consent, Wright Crittington and Keziah Crittington. Sur. Thomas Munford. p. M-1

9 April 1761. MASON, Gideon and Rebecca Walker. Sur. Edward Walker. p. M-1

9 December 1768. MASON, Launcelot and Hannah Walker, of Raleigh Parish. Sur. Edmund Walker. Launcelot Mason is of New Kent County. p. M-1

30 October 1797. MATTHEWS, Hutchens and Rebecca Jones. Sur. William Jones. p. M-4

3 November 1796. MAXEY, Bennett and Elizabeth Weldon Pride. Sur. James McGlasson. Married 3 November by Rev. James McGlasson, who says Elizabeth Weldon Pride. p. M-3 (NOTE: The Register says Elizabeth Willson Pride - the bond and Minister say Elizabeth Weldon Pride.)

16 March 1797. MAXEY, David and Lucy Hutcherson. Sur. James Hutcherson. p. M-4

74

20 September 1766. MAY, William and Betty Dyer. Sur.
Henry May. p. M-1

5 February 1789. MAYES, Garner and Judith Morris, dau.
of Moses Morris, who consents. Wit. to consent, William
Morriss and Wm. Holmes, C. A. C. Sur. J. H. Craddock.
p. M-2

-- June 1753. MAYES, John and ____ Spain. Sur. Thomas
Spain. p. M-1   (Bond mutilated.)

16 February 1789. MAYES, Robert and Agnes Theatt Locke,
dau. of Elizabeth Cordle, whose consent says, "My daughter, Agnes Thweatt Locke." Wit. to consent, John E.
Jackson and Richd Cordle. Sur. John Jackson. p. M-3

25 February 1782. MAYES, William and Lucy Johnson, who
writes her own consent. Her father, Stephen Johnson,
says she is of age. Sur. Peter Berry. p. M-2

16 September 1785. MAYES, William and Jane Fowlkes,
dau. of Gabriel Fowlkes, who consents. Sur. John Crawley. p. M-2

5 February 1789. MEADE, Everard and Mary Ward, widow.
Sur. Daniel Hardaway. p. M-3

29 October 1808. MEADE, Richard E. and Frances Bolling,
dau. of Thos. T. Bolling, whose consent says Dr. E.
Meade. Sur. Jno. R. Archer. p. M-3

5 April 1803. MEADOR, Hezekiah and Mary Avery. Sur.
Joel Avery. Married 8 April by Rev. John Pollard. p. M-3

13 January 1797. MEADOR, Jason and Polly Vaughan, dau.
of Nicholas Vaughan. Sur. Willis Vaughan. p. M-4

22 February 1810. MEADOR, Samuel and Sally Wright, dau.
of Thomas Wright, who consents. Wit. to consent, Wm.
Wright and Amos Meador. Sur. William Wright. Married
23 February by Rev. John Pollard, Senr. p. M-5

22 December 1802. MEADOR, Thomas and Nancy Johnson, dau.
of Richard Johnson. Sur. Robert Johnson. Married 23
December by Rev. John Pollard. p. M-4

25 November 1790. MEADOW, Anderson and Lucy Pollard,
dau. of Thomas Pollard, whose consent says Anderson
Meader. Wit. to consent, Ambrose Pollard and Zachary
Pollard. Sur. Waller Ford. p. M-3

23 December 1805. MEADOW, John A. and Polly Whitworth, whose Guardian is John Jeter. Sur. Jacob Whitworth. Married 23 December by Rev. John Pollard. p. M-4

17 December 1811. MEARYMOON, Jeremiah and Sarah Hood, dau. of Solomon Hood, who is surety. Nicholas Mearimoon consents, 16 December 1811, for "my son, Jeremiah Mearymoon." (Merrymoon?) Wit. to consent, Mary Eppes and Solomon Hood. Married 18 December by Rev. James Chappell. p. M-5

29 May 1797. MEREDITH, David and Elizabeth Worsham, who writes her own consent, also dated 29 May 1797. Sur. John L. Scott. p. M-3

23 November 1752. MEREDITH, Sampson and Sarah Stern. Sur. John Blanton. p. M-1

13 January 1789. MERIWEATHER, William and Ann Munford, who writes her own consent. Wit. to consent, Eliza Eggleston and Sarah Cobbs. Sur. John C. Cobbs. p. M-2

14 May 1801. MERIWEATHER, William and Sarah Scott. Sur. Joseph Scott. p. M-4

24 November 1809. MERRIN, Mathew and Sally Sneed, dau. of Claiborne Sneed. Sur. Roland Spoons. Married 28 November by Rev. Milton Robertson. p. M-4

12 December 1791. MILLER, Dabney and Polly Crowder, dau. of William Crowder, who consents. Wit. to consent, Waller Ford and Isaac Pollard. Sur. Isaac Pollard. p. M-3

5 March 1814. MILTON, John and Lucy Rucker, dau. of Sally Rucker, who consents. Wit. to consent, Pleasant Rucker and Elizabeth Rucker. Sur. Pleasant Rucker, who testifies Lucy is "upwards of 21." Wit. to bond, Benjamin Lawson, who says John Milton is of Cumberland County. Married 10 March by Rev. John Skurrey. p. M-5

16 July 1784. MITCHELL, James Cocke and Damarie Baldwin. Sur. Levi Deaton. p. M-2

19 October 1789. MITCHELL, James C. and Patience Robertson, who writes her own consent. Wit. to consent, Wm. Brooking, John Mitchell and Obedience Mitchell. Sur. John Foster. This bond is NOT in the Register.

16 March 1795. MITCHELL, James C. and Polly Craddock, who writes her own consent. Sur. Jonah Williams. p. M-3

26 January 1764. MITCHELL, John and Mary Foster. Sur. Francis Petty. Wit. to bond, Rolfe Eldridge. p. M-1

30 January 1786. MITCHELL, John and Obedience Vaughan, dau. of James Vaughan, who consents. (No wit. to consent.) Sur. James C. Mitchell. This bond is NOT in the Register.

26 January 1815. MITCHELL, Moses and Eliza F. Newby, dau. of Jesse Newby, whose consent, dated 26 January, says Rhoda Eliza F. Newby. Wit. to consent, Elizabeth Newby and Hanes Morgan. Sur. Rice Newman. Married 28 January by Rev. James Chappell. p. M-5

26 October 1791. MITCHELL, Pleasant and Rebecca Coleman, dau. of Daniel Coleman, who consents. Sur. Thos. T. Brooking. Married by Rev. John Brunskill. p. M-3

15 December 1789. MITCHELL, Thomas and Kessey Johnson, dau. of Archer Johnson, who consents. Wit. to consent, William Allen and Anderson Freeman. Sur. William Allen. Married by Rev. John Brunskill. p. M-3

5 July 1780. MITCHELL, William and Sally Price. Sur. Jos. Roach. p. M-1

14 July 1790. MOLLAY, Hugh S. and Polly Holland, who writes her own consent to Hugh S. Molloay. Wit. to consent, Peter Worsham and George Worsham. Sur. Peter Worsham. Married by Rev. John Finney. p. M-3

23 April 1813. MOODY, Benj: and Martha Marshall. John Chieves, Guardian of Martha, consents and he is surety. p. M-5

30 January 1779. MOODY, Blanks and Elizabeth Easley. Sur. John Raibourn. p. M-1

24 October 1793. MOODY, Granville and Mary Booth. Sur. Matthew Booth. p. M-4

13 June 1804. MOORE, Abel and Nancy Finney. Sur. John Webster. p. M-5

12 February 1787. MORE, Anderson and Mildred Ford. Sur. Abraham Ford. p. M-2

25 October 1804. MOORE, Joseph and Elizabeth Jones, dau. of John Jones, whose consent says Elizabeth K. Jones. Sur. David C. Jones. p. M-4

22 December 1783. MORE, Britain and Nancy Ford. Sur. John Tucker. p. M-2

24 November 1785. MOREMAN, Andrew and Prudence Hendrick, who writes her own consent. Sur. Paulin Anderson. p. M-2

2 December 1788. MOREMAN, Charles and Elizabeth Johnson, dau. of William Johnson, whose consent says "to Charles Moorman." Wit. to consent, Andrew Moorman and Jno. C. Goode. Sur. Andrew Moorman. p. M-2

5 December 1780. MORGAN, John and Ann Evans Neal. Ann Neal consents as Guardian of each. Wit. to consent, Simon Morg^n and William Morgan. Sur. Thos. S. Wells. p. M-1

25 April 1793. MORGAN, John, Sr. and Martha Tucker. Sur. Thos. T. Wills. p. M-4
(NOTE: 24th April on outside of bond - 25 April on inside of bond.)

27 August 1807. MORGAN, Simon, Jr. and Mary Newman, dau. of Elizabeth Newman. Sur. Archer Coleman. p. M-4

19 March 1787. MORING, Wyatt and Sarah Baldwin, dau. of John Baldwin, who consents and he is surety. Wit. to consent, Peter Claybrook. Married by Rev. Charles Anderson. p. M-2

22 December 1795. MORRIS, Isaac and Elizabeth Booth, dau. of Elizabeth Booth. Sur. John Chappell. p. M-4

30 January 1809. MORRIS, Joel and Sarah Holt. Sur. Robert Pollard. Married 31 January by Rev. John Skurrey. p. M-4

5 July 1791. MORRIS, John and Elizabeth Hudson, who writes her own consent. Wit. to consent, William Barding. Sur. Robert Sadler. Married by Rev. John Brunskill. p. M-3

7 July 1781. MORRIS, Moses and Elizabeth Branch Woolridge. Sur. William Claybrook. p. M-1

30 July 1796. MORRIS, Moses and Charmer Dickens (Dickerson?). Sur. James Townes. Married 1 August by Rev. James McGlasson, who says Mayre Dickens. p. M-3

20 May 1781. MORRIS, Sylvanus and Sarah Esken (Haskew?) Sur. James Cook. p. M-1
(NOTE: Sarah was widow of Joseph Haskew. See O. B. 1780 - 1782, p. 99.)

5 October 1799. MORRIS, Sylvanus and Tabitha Worsham, who writes her own consent. Wit. to consent, R. Dickey and Green Berry Worsham. Sur. Richard Dickey and David Johnson. Married 11 October by Rev. David Thomson. p. M-5

27 January 1791. MORRIS, Thomas and Lucy Ford, who writes her own consent. Wit. to consent, Waller (Walter?) Ford, who is surety. Married by Rev. John Brunskill. p. M-3

17 May 1803. MORRIS, Thomas and Judith Rogers. Married by Rev. John Pollard. Minister's Return.

16 November 1788. MORRIS, Walter and Elizabeth Morris, dau. of Silvanus Morris, who consents. Wit. to consent, Samuel C. Burton and William Johnson. Sur. Andrew Christian. p. M-2

1 July 1813. MORRIS, William O. and Anne Bell, dau. of Claiborne Bell, who consents. Wit. to consent, George Bell and William Barding. Sur. George Bell. Married 1 July by Rev. John Skurrey. p. M-5

15 December 1802. MORRIS, Zachariah and Molly Wingo, dau. of John Wingo, who is surety. Married by Rev. John Skurrey. p. M-4

24 November 1768. MORTON, John and Ann Smith. Sur. John Smith. p. M-1

26 December 1782. MORTON, Josiah and Mary Roberts. Married by Rev. Charles Anderson. Minister's Return.

29 April 1782. MOSELEY, Benjamin and Amey Giles, dau. of William Giles, who consents. Sur. John Booker. This marriage is NOT in the Register. (NOTE: Both bond and consent say Amey - not Ann.)

26 January 1809. MOSELEY, Blackman and Judith Burton, dau. of William Burton. Sur. Matthew Moseley. Married 26 January by Rev. Zachariah G. Leigh. p. M-4

16 September 1806. MOSELEY, Edward and Obedience Wilkinson. Sur. James P. Cocke. Edward Moseley is of Powhatan County. p. M-3

20 January 1784. MOSELEY, John, Jr. and Ann Willson, widow, who writes her own consent. Wit. to consent, John Finney. Sur. Edward Gibbs. p. M-2

11 November 1801. MOSELEY, Mathew and Mary Booker. Sur. John Pollard. p. M-3

3 October 1808. MOSELEY, Mathew and Martha G. Ellis. Sur. Jacob Whitworth. Married 3 October by Rev. Zachariah G. Leigh, who says Matthew Moseley. pp. M-4&5

15 December 1779. MOSELEY, William and Ann Wills. Sur.
Samuel Wills. William Moseley is of Chesterfield County.
p. M-1

28 February 1788. MOSELEY, William and Rebecca Clarke
Townes, dau. of John Townes, Sr., who consents. Sur.
William Harrison. p. M-2

13 September 1769. MOTLEY, Joel and Mary Williams, of
Nottoway Parish. Sur. Robert Vaughan, Junr. p. M-1

17 June 1783. MOTLEY, Joel and Sarah Lunsford. Sur.
Robert Vaughan. p. M-2

16 April 1785. MOTLEY, Joel and Sylvia Cook, who writes
her own consent. Wit. to consent, Fred^k Maclin and James
Cook. Sur. Matthew Robertson. p. M-2

21 December 1798. MOTTLEY, John and Polly Williams Elmore, dau. of Thomas Elmore. Sur. Parham Booker. Married
25 December by Rev. John Skurrey. p. M-4.

2 February 1808. MUNFORD, Marshall and Mary Brown.
Sur. Joseph Scott, Jr. p. M-4

11 February 1755. MUNFORD, Robert and Ann Broadnax,
niece of John Hall, who is her Guardian, and he consents.
Wit. to consent, Saml Cobbs. Sur. Samuel _____. Wit.
to bond, Samuel Pryor and Edward Munford. p. M-1

12 December 1812. MUNFORD, Thomas and Rebecca Hill.
Sur. William Booker. Married 16 December by Rev. John
Skurrey. p. M-5

1 February 1766. MUNFORD, Tho: B. and Jean ---son, of
Nottoway Parish. Sur. Richard Jones. p. M-1
(Bond is mutilated.)

11 January 1768. MUNFORD, William and Prudence Ward, of
Nottoway Parish. Sur. John Gooch. p. M-1

9 February 1793. MURRAY, Abraham and Martha Worsham,
dau. of Daniel Worsham. Sur. John Robertson. p. M-4

5 March 1790. MURRAY, Alexander and Lucy Winston, dau.
of Wm. Winston, who consents. Wit. to consent, C.
Ronald (?) and S. Booker. Sur. Samuel Winston. p. M-3
(NOTE: This bond was copied by the Clerk and noted by him
is: "Samuel Winston is either her father or brother ---
bond badly mutilated.")

2 July 1782. MURRY, Richard and Sarah Bevill. Sur.
Daniel Murry. p. M-1

28 June 1787. MURRAY, Thomas and Leonia Cannon, dau. of
William Cannon, whose consent says, "My daughter, Levina."
Wit. to consent, John Beadel and Thomas Beadel. Sur.
Augustine Beadle. p. M-2

12 February 1788. MURRAY, Thomas and Nancy Hynes. Sur.
Daniel Murray. p. M-2

8 September 1784. MURRY, William and Ridley Bevill. Sur.
Daniel Murry. p. M-2

21 October 1767. MUSE, Hopkins and Molly Wood, of this
County. Sur. William Wood. p. M-1

4 May 1784. MUSE, John and Lucy Crenshaw. Sur. Anthony
Crenshaw. p. M-2

23 March 1803. NEAL, Archer and Nancy Pollard. Sur.
John Pollard. p. N-1

22 October 1792. NEAL, Archibald and Elizabeth Berry,
dau. of Peter Berry, who consents. Sur. William Borum.
Married by Rev. John Brunskill. p. N-1

17 August 1808. NEAL, Archibald and Sally Pollard, who
writes her own consent. Wit. to consent, Thompson Scott
and Cobby Pollard. Sur. Thompson Scott. Married 18
August by Rev. John Pollard. p. N-1

17 November 1812. NEAL, Joel and Usley Coleman. George
Kidd consents for Usley. Wit. to consent, Thomas Neal
and Herod T. Crowder. Sur. Thomas Neal. Wit. to bond,
Thomas W. Powell. John Neal consents for Joel Neal.
Married 24 November by Rev. James Chappell. p. N-1

31 December 1777. NEAL, John and Anne Coleman. Sur.
Joseph Crowder. p. N-1

12 December 1808. NEAL, Thomas and Elizabeth Crowder.
Herod T. Crowder consents. Wit. to consent, William
Neal, who is surety. p. N-1

26 July 1798. NEWBY, Jesse and Judith Booth, who writes
her own consent. Wit. to consent, Matthew Booth and
Thomas Booth. Sur. Matthew Booth. p. N-1

1 March 1810. NEWBY, Jesse and Lucy Clark, who writes
her own consent. Wit. to consent, John Holt. Sur. Matthew Booth. p. N-1

26 May 1780. NICHOLSON, James and Elizabeth Fletcher.
Sur. Peter W. Robertson. p. N-1

20 December 1802. NOBLE, Austin and Frances Foster.
Sur. Richard Foster. p. N-1

27 September 1787. NOBLE, John and Susanna Wright, dau.
of John Wright, Esq., who consents. Wit. to consent,
Thos. Foster and Thos. Wright, Junr. Sur. Henry Walthall. Married by Rev. John Pollard. p. N-1

23 December 1796. NOBLE, Joshua and Oney Meadow, who
writes her own consent. Wit. to consent, Thomas Meadow
and Leroy Meador. Sur. Stephen Noble. p. N-1

17 May 1804. NORRIS, Thomas and Judith B. Rogers, dau.
of Martha Rogers, who consents. Wit. to consent, John
Wright, who is surety. Married 17 May by Rev. John Pollard. p. N-1

22 December 1785. NORVELL, William and Nancy Norton.
Sur. Edward Booker. p. N-1

14 March 1785. NUNNALLY, John and Mary Morris, dau. of
Tabitha Morris, whose consent says Mary is 22 years old.
Wit. to consent, Paulin Anderson, who is surety. p. N-1

26 February 1784. NUNNALLY, Obediah and Elizabeth Baldwin. Sur. William Baldwin. p. N-1

28 July 1803. OLD, Baxter and Nancy Coleman, dau. of
Burwell Coleman, who consents. Wit. to consent, Thomas
Worsham. Sur. Archer Coleman. p. O-1
Note on back: "Chamberlain Jones testifies that Thomas
Worsham says the inside is true."

5 February 1782. OLD, Charles and Martha Walthall, dau.
of William Walthall, who consents. Wit. to consent,
Thomas Dance. Sur. Robt. Tanner. p. O-1

19 February 1780. OLD, William and Sarah Tucker. Sur.
Robert French. p. O-1

5 August 1786. OLD, William and Winny Moore. Sur. John
Tucker. p. O-1

27 November 1759. OLIVER, John and Elizabeth Forest,
spinster, dau. of John Forest, who consents. Wit. to
consent, Richard Forrest and Abraham Forrest. Sur.
Charles Stuart. On the back of the bond: "I do certify
my son John Oliver is a free man." Signed, "James
Oliver." p. O-1

27 January 1785. OLIVER, Richard and Mary Jennings.
Sur. Joseph Jennings. p. O-1

15 June 1744. OSBORNE, William and Elizabeth Tanner.
Sur. Richard Booker. p. 0-1

12 March 1777. OSBORNE, William, Jr. and Fanny Finney,
of Raleigh Parish. Sur. William Finney. This bond is
NOT in the Register.

25 February 1812. OSBORNE, William W. and Elizabeth
Roberts, dau. of Jacob Roberts, who consents. Wit. to
consent, Robert Angel and Martha Roberts. Sur. Robert
J. Angel. p. 0-1

18 October 1783. OVERSTREET, John and Kitty Booker, who
writes her own consent. Wit. to consent, B. Overstreet
and Edward Booker, Junr. Sur. John C. Cobbs. p. 0-1

29 December 1787. OVERSTREET, John and Jenny Wood.
Sur. William Wood. Married by Rev. Charles Anderson.
p. 0-1

22 December 1778. OVERTON, Benjamin and Milly Atkinson,
dau. of Thomas Atkinson, who consents. Sur. Joshua
Atkinson. p. 0-1

23 July 1789. OVERTON, Benjamin and Elizabeth Hundley,
who writes her own consent. Wit. to consent, Joel Mottly
and James Atkinson. Sur. waller Ford. p. 0-1

8 January 1798. OVERTON, Moses and Mary Hide Booker,
widow, who writes her own consent. Sur. William Clements.
Married 10 January by Rev. John Skurrey. p. 0-1

30 March 1782. OVERTON, Thomas Purkins and Mary Ford,
dau. of Christie Ford, who consents. Wit. to consent,
Lucy Ford and Sarah Jesse. Sur. John Booker, Jr. p. 0-1

14 November 1796. OWEN, George and Fanney Clements.
Sur. Joseph Clements. p. 0-1

17 November 1798. OWEN, James and Martha Claybrook,
whose Guardian is William Morris. Sur. Zachariah Morris.
p. 0-1
"I Martha Claybrook and William Morris of Amelia do
grant James Owen leave to get a license for marriage.
Wit. Zachariah Morris and Susanna Morris."

24 December 1807. OWEN, William and Nancy Hutcheson, who
writes her own consent. Wit. to consent, William Hutcheson, who is surety. Married 26 December by Rev. John
Skurrey. p. 0-1

24 July 1783. PALMORE, Elijah and Judith Hubbard. Sur.
John Foster. p. P-1

27 November 1786. PAMPLIN, William and Fanny Jennings, dau. of Robert and Fanny Jennings, whose consent says William Pamplin is of Lunenburg County. Wit. to consent, James Jennings and Henry Jennings. Sur. William Ligon. Married by Rev. Charles Anderson. p. P-2

22 July 1784. PARHAM, Daniel and Mary Rebecca Farley. Abraham Hatchill, Rebecca's Guardian, consents. Sur. WM. Osborne. p. P-1

9 April 1792. PARKER, James and Elizabeth Howell, who writes her own consent. Wit. to consent, William Fagg and Mary Fagg. Sur. John Townes, Jr. p. P-3

25 March 1790. PATTERSON, John and Sally Lovell. Sur. Charles Lovell. p. P-2

26 December 1812. PATTERSON, William and Lucy Johnson, dau. of James Johnson, who is surety. Wit. to bond, Thos: Perkinson. p. P-3

6 November 1797. PAULET, Thomas and Mary Anderson Hughes. Her Guardian, John Royall, consents and says she is a minor. Sur. William T. Eggleston. p. P-2

19 May 1756. PAVERY, Thomas and Mary Westbrook, dau. of Wm. Westbrook, who consents. Wit. to consent, John Hardy and Rosamond Bevers. Sur. L. Claiborne. p. P-1 (NOTE: The surety signs L. Claiborne and in the top of the bond is Leonard Claiborne.)

13 April 1814. PAYNE, William P. and Sally V. Hudson. Benjamin Lawson consents "as Guardian to Sally V. Hudson." Wit. to consent, Benj: Lawson and Barbee Miller, Sur. John St. Clair. p. P-3

27 October 1785. PEARSON, David and Mary Lacy. Sur. Robert French. Married by Rev. John Goode. p. P-1

22 September 1809. PENDEL, Spencer and Nancy Waltrip, dau. of Joseph Waltrip, who consents. Wit. to consent, William Tanner and Jesse Waldrop. Sur. William Tanner. p. P-2

27 November 1788. PENNICK, Nathan and Prudence Fowlkes, dau. of Gabriel Fowlkes, who consents. (He says, "my daughter, Prudence Foultz." He signs: "Gabriel Foultz." Wit. to consent, Amey Foultz and Nathan Foultz. Sur. Gabriel Fowlkes. p. P-1

28 September 1786. PENICK, William and Mourning Fowlkes, dau. of Edward Fowlkes, who consents. Wit. to consent, Nathan Fowlkes and George Robertson. Sur. Nathan Fowlkes. p. P-1

22 July 1802. PERDUE, Paschal and Nancy W. Coleman, who writes her own consent. Wit. to consent, Allen Hood and Francis Epes. On the back of this is: "Cain Coleman gives consent to within marriage." Wit. to his consent, Allen Hood. Sur. Francis Epes. p. P-2

23 May 1806. PERKINSON, Daniel and Doratha Adams. Sur. Robert Tanner. p. P-2

29 November 1805. PERKINSON, Henry and Patience Cole. Consent for this marriage says Patience is an orphan and is signed by Jesse Waltrope and Pleasant Hood. Sur. Benjamin Tucker. p. P-2

-- ----- 1786. PERKINSON, Hezekiah and Jemima Lester, dau. of Jeremiah Lester, who consents. Consent dated 13 December 1786. Sur. Roland Lester. p. P-1

24 November 1784. PERKINSON, Jeremiah and Elizabeth Pitchford. Sur. Soloman Coleman. p. P-1

5 May 1801. PERKINSON, Joel and Elizabeth Coleman, dau. of Elizabeth Coleman, Sr., who consents. Wit. to consent, Thos. T. Wills and Robert Tanner. Sur. Robert Tanner. Married 16 May by Rev. Walthall Robertson. p. P-2

8 August 1781. PERKINSON, John Caudle and Elizabeth Bevill. Sur. Joel Hood. p. P-1

26 July 1798. PERKINSON, John, Jr. and Mary Perkinson. John Perkinson's consent says, "My daughter." Wit. to consent, Wm. Mann and Claiborne Perkinson. Sur. Claiborne Perkinson. p. P-2

3 July 1810. PERKINSON, Josiah and Fanny Jones. Sur. Edward Wilkinson. Married 15 July by Rev. Thomas Pettus. p. P-3

13 April 1783. PERKINSON, Noel and Tabitha Bevill. Sur. Joseph Roach. p. P-1

16 March 1790. PERKINSON, Thomas and Judith Clough, who writes her own consent. Sur. Richard Clough. Married by Rev. John Finney. p. P-2

3 October 1807. PERKINSON, William and Elizabeth Ann Worsham, who signs her own consent, Elizabeth A. Worsham. Wit. to consent, Simon Morgan and Hezekiah Boles. Sur. Grief Powell. p. P-2

9 August 1800. PERRY, Thomas and Lucy Perry. Married 9 August by Rev. John Pollard. Minister's Return.

4 May 1803. PERRYMAN, Anthony and Elizabeth Foster, dau. of Claiborne Foster, who consents. Wit. to consent, Wm. Fisher and John Foster. Sur. John Foster. Married 5 May by Rev. John Pollard. p. P-2

13 October 1804. PHAUP, Benjamin and Elizabeth Ellis. Patrick Henley certifies Elizabeth is 21 years old. Sur. Wm. P. Robertson. p. P-3

8 August 1781. PHILLIPS, John and Sarah Clements, dau. of Isham Clements, who consents. Sur. John Booker. p. P-1

6 August 1782. PHILLIPS, Rhody and Ann Isbell. Sur. Luke Lipscomb. Rhody is son of Thomas Phillips, who consents. Wit. to consent, Luke Lipscomb, Ellis Evans and James Hollingsworth. p. P-1

29 May 1778. PHILLIPS, Richard and Elizabeth Clements, dau. of Isham Clements, who consents. Wit. to consent, Joshua Chaffin and Richard Holt. Sur. Richard Holt. p. P-1

13 December 1785. PHILLIPS, William and Mary Easley Winfree. Sur. John Wingo. Married by Rev. Charles Anderson, who says Mary Easley Winfrey. Returned 24 August 1786. p. P-1

15 April 1782. PILES, Conradus and Eleanor Jackson, dau. of William Jackson, who consents. Sur. William Howlett. Married by Rev. Jeremiah Walker. p. P-1

22 February 1812. PILLER, Dearen and Dicey Coleman, dau. of Archer Coleman, who consents and says Darien Pillar. Wit. to consent, Thomas Worsham and John Piller. Sur. Thomas Worsham. Married 26 February by Rev. James Chappell. p. P-3

5 January 1761. PINCHAM, Peter and Elizabeth Dennis, dau. of Richard Dennis, who consents. Wit. to consent, Rich'd Dennis, Junr. and Martha Dennis. Sur. Richard Dennis, Junr. p. P-1

18 December 1786. PINCHAM, Samuel and Sophia Sherwin, dau. of Samuel Sherwin, who consents. Wit. to consent, Jno. Royall and Wm. Greenhill. Sur. Phillip W. Greenhill. p. P-1

20 April 1810. PITCHFORD, Laban and Juda Pennell. Joseph Waltrip consents. Wit. to consent, Jesse Waltrip and Juda Pennell. Sur. Joseph Waltrip. Married 21 April by Rev. James Chappell, who says Judith. p. P-3

23 October 1785. PITCHFORD, Samuel and Elener Hall.
(Eleanor?). Sur. Archer Johnson. p. P-1

27 April 1780. POINDEXTER, Johnathan and Mary Ashley.
Sur. James Scott. p. P-1

7 December 1791. POLLARD, Benjamin and Sally Johnson,
dau. of Nicholas Johnson, who consents. Wit. to consent,
John Wright and Elizabeth Berry. Sur. William Johnson.
Married 13 December by Rev. Abner Watkins. p. P-2

21 December 1786. POLLARD, Francis and Patty Johnson,
dau. of Stephen Johnson, who consents. Wit. to consent,
Walter Morriss and Barnard Hendrick. Sur. William Pollard. p. P-2

24 February 1791. POLLARD, Francis and Patty Scott, who
writes her own consent. Wit. to consent, William Pollard
and Paulin Anderson. Sur. Paulin Anderson. p. P-2

10 March 1786. POLLARD, James and Polly Foster, dau. of
Thomas Foster, Jr., whose consent is dated 4 March 1786.
Sur. Peter Berry. p. P-1

5 January 1815. POLLARD, John and Polly A. Neal, dau. of
John Neal, who consents. Wit. to consent, John Neal and
Thomas Neal. Sur. Joel Neal. Married 7 January by Rev.
James Chappell. p. P-3

14 December 1807. POLLARD, Joseph and Elizabeth Coleman,
who writes her own consent. Wit. to consent, William
Coleman, Braxton Coleman and Thomas Neal. Sur. Braxton
Coleman. p. P-2

30 November 1798. POLLARD, Moses and Nancy Morris. Sur.
Isaac Morris. p. P-2

26 November 1812. POLLARD, Robert and Mahala Chapman,
dau. of Benjamin Chapman, who consents. Wit. to consent,
John Chapman, Oney Chapman, Chiller Ray Chapman and P. H.
Chapman. Sur. Patrick H. Chapman. p. P-3

2 June 1781. POLLARD, Thomas and Mary Pollard. Sur.
Joseph Pollard. p. P-1

1 November 1788. POLLARD, Thomas and Dorothea Robertson. Sur. Peter W. Robertson. p. P-2

3 July 1794. POLLARD, Thomas and Mary Asselin, who
writes her own consent. Sur. Francis Asselin. Married 4 July by Rev. James McGlasson. p. P-2

22 December 1787. POLLARD, William and Keziah Seay, who
writes her own consent. Wit. to consent, Paulin Anderson
and Anney Seay. Sur. Thos: Morris. p. P-1

19 February 1788. POLLARD, Zachariah and Rhoda Johnson,
dau. of Stephen Johnson, who consents. Wit. to consent,
William May, who is surety. Married by Rev. John Pollard. p. P-1

27 December 1797. PONTON, Edward and Elizabeth Deshazer,
who writes her own consent. Wit. to consent, Jas.
Vaughan and Peter Ponton. Sur. Peter Ponton. p. P-2

30 August 1806. PONTON, John and Lucy Robertson, who
writes her own consent. Sur. Ed Land. p. P-2

29 May 1800. PONTON, Peter and Lucy Vaughan, who writes
her own consent. Wit. to consent, Ben Overstreet, who
is surety. p. P-2

10 October 1786. PORTER, James May and Elizabeth Robertson, dau. of John Robertson, who consents. Wit. to consent, Thomas Bass and Richd Smith. Sur. Thomas Beasley.
James May is son of James May Porter, deceased. Nathaniel Robertson consents. Wit. to his consent, William
And^s Morris and William Robertson. Married by Rev.
Charles Anderson. p. P-2

1 May 1784. POVALL, John and Elizabeth Johnson. Sur.
John Royall, Jr. p. P-1

27 December 1781. POWELL, Abraham and Frances Bevill.
Sur. John Powell. p. P-1

6 April 1808. POWELL, Grief and Elizabeth Walden. Consent of Elizabeth Walden, who says each is of age. Wit.
to consent, Thos: Bragg, who is surety. p. P-3

7 December 1785. POWELL, John and Sarah Perkinson. Sur.
Field Perkinson. p. P-1

20 April 1797. POWELL, Richard and Martha Coleman. Sur.
Jordan Hood. p. P-2

15 October 1796. POWELL, Robert and Sally Coleman. Sur.
Jos: Coleman. p. P-2

8 January 1803. POWELL, Thomas and Rebecca Markham. Her
Guardian, Henry Branch, consents. Wit. to consent, N.
Patterson and M. Townes, Jr. Sur. Nelson Patterson. Mar-
ried 13 January by Rev. John Skurrey. p. P-2

19 December 1815. POWELL, Thos. W. and Martha A. Leigh.
Sur. J. T. Leigh.   p. P-3

23 December 1788. POWELL, William and Ann Paulin Anderson, who writes her own consent. Wit. to consent, James McGlasson and Mildred McGlasson. Sur. J. D. Gunn. Married 1 January 1789 by Rev. John Finney. p. P-1

3 August 1793. POWELL, William and Hannah Perkinson.
Sur. Field Perkinson. p. P-3

23 August 1781. PRICE, Charles and Betsy Fowlkes. Sur.
John Fowlkes. Married 25 August by Rev. Jeremiah Walker.
p. P-1

10 October 1784. PRICE, William and Elizabeth Littlepage.
Sur. L. Hudson. p. P-1   (In top of bond is Lew J. hudson.)

19 August 1801. PRIDE, John, Jr. and Elizabeth G. Worsham. Sur. James Townes, Jr. Married by Rev. David Thomson. p. P-2

30 January 1799. PRIDE, Thomas and Rebecca Pride. Sur.
John Pride. Married 30 January by Rev. Bennett (?)
Maxey. p. P-2

2 March 1814. PRIDE, Thomas and Harriet Anderson, who writes her own consent. Thomas Pride and Thos. Wily testify she is 21. Sur. Wood Jones. Married 3 March by Rev. John Skurrey. p. P-3
(NOTE: Is this a double wedding? See Jones Wood.)

31 August 1764. PRIDE, William and Mary Towns. Sur.
John Booker. p. P-1

25 March 1789. PUGH, John and Sally Hundley, who writes her own consent. Wit. to consent, John Harper and Charles D. George. Sur. John Harper. p. P-2

22 November 1815. QUENICHET, Vivant and Lucy Marshall, who requests this license. Benj. Moody testifies Lucy is 21 and he is surety. Married 22 November by Rev.
James Chappell. p. Q-1

7 March 1768. RAGSDALE, Robert and Judith Hudson, widow, of this County. Sur. Munford Willson. p. R-1

12 November 1806. RAINES, James and Sally Noble, dau. of Joseph Noble, who consents. Wit. to consent, Elizabeth P----- and William Rains. Sur. William Rains. Married 13 November by Rev. John Pollard. p. R-3

11 September 1786. RAMSEY, Booker and Elizabeth Munford.
On 7 September 1786, John Munford, Guardian of Elizabeth,
writes consent for Booker Ramsey to marry "Miss Ann
Elizabeth Munford." Wit. to consent, William H. Munford.
Sur. Zenel Ramsey. p. R-2

24 June 1784. RAMSAY, Henry and Polly Williamson. Sur.
Lewelling Williamson. p. R-2

18 November 1800. RANDOLPH, Bathurst and Mary Tabb, dau.
of Frances Tabb, who consents. Wit. to consent, Frances
Cook Tabb and Anderson _____. Sur. Francis Anderson.
p. R-2

17 September 1778. RANDOLPH, Peter and Sarah Greenhill.
Sur. Thos: Williams. p. R-1

15 March 1806. RANDOLPH, Peyton and Marian Ward. Sur.
Joseph Eggleston. p. R-3
(NOTE: The Register has Mariah - the bond has Marian.)

8 November 1802. READ, John and Martha B. Townes, dau.
of John Townes, Sr., who consents. Sur. James Townes,
Jr. Married 8 November by Rev. David Thomson. p. R-3

12 June 1780. REAMS, Frederick and Martha Ann Berry.
Sur. Thos: Belcher. p. R-1

11 July 1764. REDFORD, Andrew and Mary Jones, spinster,
dau. of Edward Jones, deceased. Daniel James, Mary's
Guardian, consents. Sur. Jesse Lunsford. p. R-1

1 February 1768. REES, Isham and Rhoda Thomas. Sur.
William Thomas. p. R-1

22 February 1759. REES, James and Margaret Lewis, spinster, dau. of George Lewis. Sur. Thomas Claiborne.
p. R-1

15 October 1784. REESE, Jesse and Susanna Roach. Sur.
John Roach. This bond is NOT in the Register.

27 October 1803. REESE, Parham and Nancy Chandler. Sur.
Martin Chandler. p. R-2

24 October 1759. RICE, James and Jean Wallace, under 21,
dau. of Mary Wallace, who consents. Wit. to consent,
Chas. Irby and John Wallis. Sur. John Wallis. p. R-1

23 April 1761. RICHARDSON, Ruler and Ann Hulme. Sur.
Richard Hulme. p. R-1

15 January 1789. RICHARDSON, Ruler and Amey Fowlks, who writes her own consent. Wit. to consent, George Robertson and James Anderson. Sur. Isham Clay. p. R-2

2 December 1815. RICHARDSON, Thomas and Martha Hill, who writes her own consent. Her father, James Hill, also consents. Sur. David Goodwin, who testifies Martha is of age. Married 2 December by Rev. George Robertson. p. R-3

26 February 1789. RICHARDSON, William and Rebecca Green, dau. of John Green, who consents. Wit. to consent, _____ Davis and Reinard Anderson. Sur. T. Gunn (Green?) p. R-2

15 November 1806. RICHERSON, Elisha and Frankey Dearin, dau. of William Dearin, who is surety. Married 20 November by Rev. John Skurrey. p. R-3

19 February 1780. RISEN (Rison?), Elery and Elizabeth Rowlet, dau. of George Rowlett, who is surety. p. R-1

7 November 1808. RISON, Ellery and Frances Vasser. Sur. Mertel Leseur. p. R-2

28 December 1802. RISON, John and Jane Foster. Sur. John Foster. p. R-2

17 January 1814. RISON, Peter and Sally B. Booker, who writes her own consent. Wit. to consent, Wm. Booker and Jno. C. Hill. Sur. Jno. C. Hill. Married 17 January by Rev. John Skurrey. p. R-3

21 December 1793. RISON, Richard and Polly Rison, dau. of William Ponton, who consents. Wit. to consent, John Ponton and Edward Ponton. Sur. Ellery Rison. p. R-2

4 February 1789. RIVERS, Robert and Betiah Eckles. Sur. James Eckles. p. R-2

13 May 1801. RIVES, Anthony and Mary Green, dau. of Abraham Green, who consents. Wit. to consent, Rachel Cousins and Jno. Hamlin. Sur. John Hamlin. p. R-2

23 July 1761. RIVES, Frederick and Magdalin Stegall. George Stegall's consent, dated 23 July 1761, says, "my daughter, Mary Magdeline Stegall." Wit. to consent, Thomas Young and B_____ Stegall. Sur. George Stegall. p. R-1
(NOTE: The Register says 28 June - bond and consent say 23 July.)

28 August 1764. RIVES, Thomas and Eleanor Neal, spinster. Sur. David Neal. p. R-1

16 October 1784. ROACH, John and Betsy Rees. Amey Rees, Guardian of Betsey Reese, consents. Consent dated, 16 October 1784. Wit. to consent, James Clark and William Clark. Sur. Abel Mann.

18 April 1815. ROACH, Millington D. and Prudence Talley, dau. of Peyton Talley, who consents. Consent dated, 18 April 1815. Wit. to consent, Woodley Talley and Grief B. Hawkins. Sur. Grief B. Hawkins. Married 24 April by Rev. James Chappell. p. R-3

29 September 1790. ROACH, William and Eliza Hood. Sur. Abel Mann. Married 8 October by Rev. Robert Marshall, who says, William Roach, Planter. p. R-2

25 April 1811. ROBERTS, Chastain and Polly Adams, who writes her own consent. Wit. to consent, George W. Farley and Matthew Farley. Sur. Geo. W. Farley, who testifies Polly "is upwards of 21." p. R-3

22 November 1781. ROBERTS, Jacob and Magdalin Hudson. Sur. Alex. Roberts. p. R-1

19 November 1750. ROBERTS, James and Susanna Ellis, dau. of John Ellis, Senr., who consents. Wit. to consent, Richard Ellis and William Roberts. Sur. Richard Ellis. p. R-1

27 October 1796. ROBERTS, John and Betsy Farley. Sur. Mathew Farley. p. R-3

20 December 1815. ROBERTS, John and Sally Jeter, dau. of Allen Jeter, who consents. Wit. to consent, Edward Berry, who is surety. Married 21 December by Rev. John Skurrey. p. R-3

19 December 1782. ROBERTS, William and Sally Holt. Married by Rev. Charles Anderson. Minister's Return.

28 March 1792. ROBERTS, William and Rebecca Tucker. Sur. Thomas Hood. p. R-3

10 August 1795. ROBERTSON, Archer, Junr. and Frances Brooking, dau. of Robt. Edward Brooking, deceased. Her Guardian, V. Brooking, consents. Wit. to consent, Edwd. B. Brooking and Francis Brooking. Sur. Francis Brooking. p. R-2

20 July 1805. ROBERTSON, Archer and Nancy M. Booker, who writes her own consent. Wit. to consent, John C. Booker, who is surety. p. R-2

27 April 1809. ROBERTSON, Archer and Sarah Marshall, who writes her own consent. Wit. to consent, John Walthall. Sur. James Robertson. p. R-2

20 October 1808. ROBERTSON, Daniel and Page F. Bowles, dau. of Henry Bowles, whose consent says, "my daughter, Page Finney Bowles." Wit. to consent, Matthew Booth and Hezekiah Bowles. Sur. Hezekiah Bowles. Married 29 October by Rev. William Dier. p. R-2

2 February 1782. ROBERTSON, Edward and Mary Pulliam Thomson. Married by Rev. Jeremiah Walker. Returned 2 May 1782. Minister's Return.

20 March 1769. ROBERTSON, Francis and Lucretia Townes, dau. of William Townes, who consents. Wit. to consent, W. Townes, Jr. and John Pride. Sur. William Townes. p. R-1

10 July 1779. ROBERTSON, George and Nancey Anderson,dau. of John Anderson, who is surety. p. R-1

21 December 1786. ROBERTSON, George and Betsy Bagley, dau. of Dicey Bagley, whose consent says, "my daughter, Bettey Bagley." Wit. to consent, Nathan Fowlkes, James Bagley and Anderson Jennings. Sur. Anderson Jennings. p. R-2

28 February 1805. ROBERTSON, George and Christian Bass. Sur. James Robertson and Edward Bass. This bond is NOT in the Register.

1 April 1762. ROBERTSON, Henry and Tralucia Greenwood, widow. Sur. Ambrose Estes. p. R-1

24 September 1805. ROBERTSON, Henry W. and Susana B. Ellison. Sur. Edward Bass. p. R-3

2 October 1798. ROBERTSON, James, Jr. and Mary Epes Robertson, dau. of John Robertson. Sur. Peterfield Archer. p. R-2

31 July 1776. ROBERTSON, John and Elizabeth Royall, dau. of John Royall, whose consent is dated 30 July 1776. Wit. to consent, John Royall and John Robertson. Sur. John Royall, Junr. p. R-1

8 April 1786. ROBERTSON, John and Betty Branch Robertson, who writes her own consent. Sur. John Archer. p. R-2

30 June 1803. ROBERTSON, John, Jr. and Elizabeth Booker. Sur. John S. Booker. p. R-3

27 April 1809. ROBERTSON, John R. and Mary E. Robertson, who writes her own consent. Wit. to consent, J. Robertson, Jr. Sur. James Robertson, Jr. p. R-2

8 August 1812. ROBERTSON, Lloyd and Polly Craddock Jackson, dau. of Abel Jackson, who consents. Wit. to consent, Wright E. Noble and Claiborne Craddock. Sur. Claiborne Craddock. Married 9 August by Rev. John Skurrey. p. R-3

25 May 1785. ROBERTSON, Matthew and Elizabeth Hurt, who writes her own consent. Wit. to consent, John Mitchel and Joel Mottley. Sur. Joel Mottley. p. R-2

25 January 1785. ROBERTSON, Robert and Molly May Porter, who writes her own consent. Wit. to consent, William May Porter and Mary May Porter. Sur. James Robertson. Nathaniel Robertson consents for son Robert, dated 1 January 1785. Wit. to his consent, William May Porter and Mary May Porter. Nathaniel Robertson, Executor for her father, deceased, consents for her. Consent dated 1 January 1785. p. R-2

21 October 1777. ROBERTSON, William and Betty Branch Worsham. William Giles consents for Betty Branch Worsham. Wit. to consent, John Robertson and William Giles. Sur. William Worsham. p. R-1

7 March 1793. ROBERTSON, William and Catharine Ford. Sur. Robert Farguson. p. R-3 See: William Robertson.

23 March 1793. ROBERTSON, William and Cynthia Ford, dau. of W. Ford, who consents on 2 March 1793 and says, "my daughter, Cynthia. Wit. to consent, Hezekiah Ford and Robert Farguson. Married 23 March by Rev. James McGlasson. This is consent and Minister's Return. See: William Robertson.

21 July 1806. ROBINSON, T. and Anne Murray, who writes her own consent to Thos. Robinson. Sur. Ben Overstreet. The groom signs Thos. Robinson. p. R-2

14 October 1783. ROGERS, William and Hannah Dickson Seay. Sur. Abraham Seay. p. R-1 See: William Rogers.

14 October 1783. ROGERS, William and Hannah Dix, dau. of Hannah Dix, who consents. Wit. to consent, Wm. Rogers and Abraham Seay. This is consent ONLY. See: William Rogers.

3 April 1779. ROKE, Hugh and Susanna Wilkerson, of Nottoway Parish. Sur. John Drinkard. Wit. to bond, Zachariah Hawkins and James Wilkerson. p. R-1

25 March 1788. RONALDS, William and Christiana Winston, dau. of William Winston, who consents. Wit. to consent, Lucy Winston and John Winston. Sur. Sam'l Winston. William Ronalds is of Powhatan County. p. R-2

24 March 1806. RONALS, Hezekiah and Elizabeth Raines, who writes her own consent to Hezekiah Ronals. Wit. to consent, Wm. Wright, Pleasant Seay and William Hudson. Sur. William Wright. Married 22 December by Rev. John Pollard. p. R-2
(NOTE: The Register says Rauls - the bond, consent and Minister's Return say Ronals.)

23 November 1809. ROSS, Daniel and Delilah Foster. Sur. John W. Foster. p. R-2

19 December 1801. ROWLAND, Absalom and Amy Hurt. Married by Rev. John Pollard. Minister's Return.

27 January 1814. ROWLETT, George and Martha O. Mann. Sur. Daniel Mann. p. R-3

31 December 1750. ROYALL, John and Elizabeth Worsham. Sur. Stith Hardaway. p. R-1

26 February 1777. ROYALL, John and Sarah Dennis, of Raleigh Parish. Sur. John Archer. John Royall is of Chesterfield County. p. R-1

1 May 1784. ROYALL, John, Jr. and Betty Townes. Sur. John Powell. p. R-1

13 December 1800. ROYALL, Joseph A. and Hannah W. Finney, who writes her own consent to Joseph A. Royall. Wit. to consent, ___ Robertson and James T. Royall. Sur. James T. Royall. p. R-3

25 May 1780. ROYALL, Littleberry and Elizabeth Jones. Sur. Richard Hayes. p. R-1

3 August 1795. ROYALL, Richard and Mary C. Hudson. Her Guardian, Richard Booker, consents. Consent dated 3 August 1795. Wit. to consent, Edward Scott and John C. Cobbs. Sur. Edward Scott. p. R-3

9 January 1805. ROYALL, William and Judith Archer Royall. John Royall consents. Wit. to consent, Jos. A. Royall and Jas. T. Royall. Sur. Jos. A. Royall. p. R-3

9 February 1762. RUCKER, Gideon and Elizabeth Cook, dau. of John Cook, who consents. Wit. to consent, James Tinsley, who is surety. p. R-1

5 December 1808. RUCKER, Pleasant and Betsy Farley. Sur. Wm. Farley. Married 5 December by Rev. John Skurrey. p. R-3

20 December 1793. RUCKER, Reuben and Susannah Kelly, dau. of Ellick Z. Kelly, who consents. Wit. to consent, Zachariah Hendrake and Joshua Rucker. Sur. Joshua Rucker. Married by Rev. James McGlasson. p. R-2

18 December 1792. RUCKER, Samuel and Polly Rucker. Sur. Joshua Rucker. Married by Rev. John Brunskill. p. R-2

1 February 1779. RUDD, Aldridge and Ann Hawkins. Sur. David Hawkins. Aldridge Rudd is of Chesterfield County. p. R-1

23 October 1779. RUDD, Hezekiah and Lucy Hawkins. Sur. David Hawkins. p. R-1

19 October 1812. RUDD, John, Jr. and Frances R. Mann, dau. of Joel Mann, who consents. Wit. to consent, William Clark and William Newman. Sur. William Clark. Married 21 October by Rev. James Chappell. p. R-3

3 June 1803. RUDD, Samuel and Nancy Bass, who writes her own consent. Wit. to consent, Mary Bass and Lewellin Hudson. Sur. Lewellyn Hudson. Married 18 June by Rev. James Rucker. p. R-2

31 December 1782. SADLER, James and Matilda Hurt, dau. of Wm. Hurt, who consents. Sur. Wm. Ham. p. S-1

30 May 1809. SADLER, John and Nancy Hubbard, whose Guardian, Robert Sadler, is surety. Married 31 May by Rev. John Pollard, who says Mary Hubbard. P. S-2
On the back of the bond is: "Rev. Robert Sadler."
This is signed, "J. Townes."

5 July 1791. SADLER, Robert and Rachel Hubbard, who writes her own consent. Wit. to consent, William Barding. Sur. John Morris. Married by Rev. John Brunskill. p. S-2

23 December 1789. SADLER, Samuel and Mary Hurt, dau. of William Hurt, Sr., who consents. Wit. to consent, W. Williamson and Abr^m Min-----. Sur. William Ham. p. S-2

25 April 1793. SANDEFER, Mathew and Mary Johnston Wills. Sur. Thomas T. Wills. p. S-3

26 December 1815. SANFORD, James and Elizabeth Brewer.
Married by Rev. James Chappell. Minister's Return.

25 May 1775. SAUNDERS, John Hyde and Rachel Bentley.
Sur. George Hancock, Jr. John Hyde Saunders is of Chesterfield County. p. S-1

11 February 1795. SAYRE, Daniel and Sylvia Mottley, who
writes her own consent to "the Beaver Doct^r D. Sayre."
Wit. to consent, James C. Mitchell, who is surety. p. S-3

29 January 1806. SCHULTZ, John and Lucy Willson. Sur.
Richard Wilson. Married by Rev. John Pollard. p. S-2

25 November 1790. SCOTT, Edward and Mary Jones, who
writes her own consent. Wit. to consent, Sam Booker and
Wm. M. Booker. Sur. Samuel Booker. Married by Rev. John
Finney. p. S-2

22 December 1814. SCOTT, George L. and Clarkey Ann Webster, whose Guardian, John Rison, consents. Wit. to consent, W. E. Noble. Sur. P. L. Townes. Married 27 December by Rev. John Skurrey. p. S-4

23 December 1809. SCOTT, James and Elizabeth H. Mann,
dau. of Joel Mann, whose consent is dated 23 December
1809. Sur. Samuel Scott. Married 28 December by Rev.
James Chappell. p. S-3
(NOTE: The Register says 4 September - bond and consent
are dated 23 December.)

7 September 1759. SCOTT, John and Sarah Scott. Sur.
Robert Jones. p. S-1

16 January 1783. SCOTT, John and L(ucy) W(orsham). Sur.
Alex. Walker. George Covington, on 1 January 1783, consents for John Scott, infant son of John Scott, to marry
Lucy Worsham. Wit. to consent, Wm. N. Booker and Allen
Burton. p. S-2

8 March 1814. SCOTT, John F. and Oney Wright, whose
Guardian, John Jeter, consents. (Consent says John F.
Scott.) Wit. to consent, Bernard Jeter Seay and Daniel
Booker. Sur. Bernard Seay. Married 10 March by Rev.
John Pollard. p. S-4

21 September 1788. SCOTT, John Lawson and Mary Worsham,
dau. of Phoebe Worsham, who consents. Wit. to consent,
Peter Worsham and George Worsham. Sur. Richard Foster.
p. S-2

13 November 1778. SCOTT, Joseph, Jr. and Elizabeth
Booker, whose Guardian, Richard Booker writes his consent
from Charlotte, Virginia. Wit. to consent, Wm. M. Booker
and Allen Burton. Sur. Peter R. Booker. Jacob Williamson, Guardian of Joseph, consents. Wit. to his consent,
Jacob Williamson and David Sudberry. p. S-1

10 November 1803. SCOTT, Joseph and Caroline Booker.
Sur. John Robertson. Married 10 November by Rev. William
Dier. p. S-3

-- April 1758. SCOTT, Roger and Prudence Farley, dau. of
Henry Farley, whose consent is dated 28 April 1758. Wit.
to consent, Francis Jackfon and George Farley. Sur.
George Farley. p. S-1

18 December 1798. SCOTT, Thompson and Nancy Chaffin,
dau. of Joshua Chaffin, whose consent is dated 13 December 1798. Wit. to consent, Tinsley Chaffin and Archibald Neal. Sur. Tinsley Chaffin. Married 20 December by
Rev. John Skurrey. p. S-3

15 October 1804. SCRUGGS, William and Frances Wingo,
dau. of John Wingo, who is surety. p. S-4

9 February 1801. SEAY, Austin and Sally M. Booker, who
writes her own consent, dated: 9 February 1801. Her
mother, Mary Booker, also consents, and says Sally Marshall Booker. Sur. Samuel Ford, who witnesses both of
above consents. Married 28 February by Rev. John Skurrey. p. S-2

28 June 1792. SEAY, Cyrus and Nancy Wingo. Sur. Josiah
Seay. p. S-3

9 July 1791. SEAY, Dudley and Rachel Smith Seay, dau. of
Frances and John Wingo, who request the license. Sur.
Abraham Seay. Married by Rev. John Brunskill. p. S-2

9 August 1784. SEAY, Jacob and Mary Bagley. Dicy Bagley consents. Wit. to consent, Edmund Bowen, Peter Grigg
and Worsham Anderson. Sur. John Seay. p. S-2

21 November 1791. SEAY, Jacob and Rebecca Jenkins, dau.
of James Jenkins, who consents. Wit. to consent, Zachary
Ford and James Hillsman. Sur. Samuel Ford. Married by
Rev. John Brunskill. p. S-2

22 March 1792. SEAY, James and Anne Hatchett, dau. of
Isaiah Hatchett, who consents. Wit. to consent, John
Wingo and Thomas Burton. Sur. John Hatchett. p. S-3

10 June 1783. SEAY, John and Ann Hillsman. Sur. Edward
Munford. p. S-1

16 December 1806. SEAY, Pleasant and Elizabeth Hudson,
whose Guardian, Joshua Smithey, consents. Wit. to consent, Robert L. Smithey and Asey Foster. Sur. Asey
Jeter. p. S-3

21 May 1798. SELDEN, John W. and Ann Booker. Sur.
Daniel Booker. p. S-3

10 December 1779. SELF, Thomas and Oney Ham. Sur. Jacob
Belcher. p. S-1

4 October 1806. SHEFFIELD, Stephen and Nancy Ann Jack-
son, dau. of Moses Jackson, whose consent is dated 11
August, 1806. Wit. to consent, James Hill. Sur. Moses
Jackson. p. S-2

29 January 1760. SHELTON, Abraham and Cloe Robertson,
dau. of Henry Robertson, who consents. Wit. to consent,
Wm. Hudson and Henry Hudson. Sur. John Harper. p. S-1

28 October 1785. SHELTON, Crispin, Jr. and Susannah Irby,
who writes her own consent. Wit. to consent, Nathan Fletcher and Will. Shelton. Sur. Peter Robertson. p. S-2

24 March 1762. SHELTON, Gabriel and Elizabeth Shepherd,
who writes her own consent. Wit. to consent, James Johnson and Letty Johnson. Sur. Abraham Shelton. p. S-1

27 December 1777. SHELTON, Vincent and Susanna Robertson,
dau. of Henry Robertson, who consents. Wit. to consent,
Crispin Robertson and Leonard Shelton. Sur. Abraham
Mottley. Vincent is son of Crispen Shelton, of Pittsyl-
vania County, who consents. Wit. to his consent, Beverly
Shelton and Gabriel Shelton. p. S-1

26 May 1806. SHORT, Samuel and Berry Anderson. Sur.
Francis Goodwin. p. S-3

23 September 1762. SHORT, Thomas and Dorothy Jones.
Sur. Peter Jones, Junr. p. S-1

29 November 1787. SHORT, Thomas, Jr. and Martha Jones,
dau. of John Jones, who consents. Wit. to consent, Thos.
S. Jones and Peter Branch. Sur. Thomas S. Jones. p. S-2

7 December 1761. SIMMONS, Benjamin and Martha Simmons,
whose consent is dated 2 December 1761. Sur. William
Whitehead. p. S-1

14 March 1801. SIMMONS, Thomas and Martha A. Jones, dau. of John Jones, whose consent says Thomas Simmons is of Brunswick County. Wit. to consent, Drury Jones and John Jones. Sur. Drury Jones. p. S-3

20 January 1786. SIMMONS, William and Grisel Edmundson. Sur. Richard Edmundson. p. S-2

29 June 1808. SKIPWITH, George N. and Mary Murray, dau. of William Murray, who consents. Wit. to consent, Mary B. Anderson and Thomas Murray. Sur. Edmund Harrison. p. S-3

21 May 1814. SKURREY, John and Susanna Walton, who writes her own consent, dated 21 May. Wit. to consent, Boswell Traylor, who testifies she is "of full age" and he is surety. Married 22 May by Rev. W. H. Pitman, Baptist. p. S-4

25 January 1787. SMITH, Griffin and Mary Ellis, who writes her own consent. Wit. to consent, John Crute. Sur. Thomas Ellis. Married by Rev. Simeon Walton. p. S-2

3 November 1807. SMITH, Joel and Prudence Bridgewater, who writes her own consent. Sur. Polly Bottom. p. S-3

-- ------ ----. SMITH, John and Frances Arms. Married by Rev. John Brunskill. Minister's Return. This report has no date.

24 September 1799. SMITH, John and Jincey McCann (Machan?). John Machan consents for "John Smith to marry Jinsey Machan." Wit. to consent, Raleigh Stott, who is surety. Married 25 September by Rev. John Skurrey, who says Janey McCann. p. S-3
(Bond and Minister's Return say McCann - consent has Machan.)

9 March 1810. SMITH, Joseph and Judith Townes. Sur. James Booker. p. S-4

5 August 1793. SMITH, Lindsey and Molly Bailey, who writes her own consent. Martha Bailey, her mother, also consents. Sur. Abram Bailey. p. S-3

20 May 1785. SMITH, Samuel and Elizabeth Jordan. Mary Jordan, of Nottoway Parish, consents and says Elizabeth is under 21. Wit. to consent, Sam Jordan and Thos. Jordan. Sur. Batt Cocke. p. S-2

30 April 1776. SMITH, Thomas and Tabitha Williamson, dau. of Jacob Williamson, whose consent says Thomas is of Hanover County. Wit. to consent, William Harrison, who is surety. p. S-1

19 June 1807. SMITH, Thomas and Rebecca Farley, dau. of Mathew Farley, who consents. Sur. Peter Farley. p. S-3

23 January 1783. SMITH, William and "not filled in". Sur. Daniel Parham. p. S-1

13 September 1806. SMITH, William and Betsy F. Carter. Sur. Jesse Walton. Married 15 September by Rev. H. Wood. p. S-3

3 December 1785. SMITH, William and Mary Raglin. Sur. Joseph Raglin. Married 13 December by Rev. Devereux Jarratt, who says Mary Ragland. p. S-2

20 October 1810. SMITH, William and Elizabeth Stringer, who writes her own consent. Wit. to consent, Philip Dunnavant and James Stringer. Sur. James Stringer, who testifies Elizabeth is of age. p. S-4

14 April 1802. SMITHEY, John M. and Manner Meadows. Sur. Thos. Meadows. p. S-3

25 January 1810. SMITHEY, Robert L. and Parthena Foster, who writes her own consent. Wit. to consent, John W. Smithey, Richard Foster and Richard W. Ligon. Sur. Richard W. Ligon. Married 30 January by Rev. John Pollard, Senr. p. S-4

4 January 1786. SNEED, Samuel and Patsy Clay. Sur. Charles Clay. p. S-2

27 August 1795. SOUTHALL, Henry H. and Nancy Tanner, dau. of Blanch Tanner, who consents. Wit. to consent, Stephen Southall and Ebenezer Coleman, who, together, are surety. p. S-3

28 March 1805. SOUTHALL, John and ____ ____. Sur. Jesse Martin. p. S-2

23 June 1808. SOUTHALL, John and Polly Hall, who writes her own consent. Wit. to consent, H. Holeman Southall and Jesse Southall. Sur. John Eppes. p. S-4

25 August 1796. SOUTHALL, Stephen and Elizabeth Clay. Sur. Henry H. Southall. p. S-4

XXVIII December 1757. SOWELL, Thomas and Oney Johnson, spinster. John Wright, her Guardian, consents on Decr XXVIII, L757 and says she is an orphan. Wit. to consent, Gerrard Ellyson and William Johnson. Sur. William Johnson. p. S-1

16 August 1760. SPAIN, David and Abigail Roberts, dau. of J. Roberts, who consents. Wit. to consent, John Baldwin and William Baldwin. Sur. John A. Baldwin. p. S-1

23 March 1792. SPAIN, Epes and Doretha Chappell, who signs her consent, Dorothy Chappell to Epes Spain, jr. Wit. to consent, Wm. Howlett and James Howlett. Sur. Wm. Howlett. p. S-3

28 May 1761. SPAIN, Francis and Elinor Truly. Sur. Benjamin Branch. p. S-1

-- March 1772 (52?). SPAIN, Frederick and Mary Roberts. Sur. Nicholas Brown. p. S-1   (Bond is mutilated.)

15 December 1788. SPAIN, Newman and Catey Crenshaw. Sur. William Crenshaw. Married 20 December by Rev. John Finney. p. S-2

25 July 1754. SPAIN, Thomas and Elizabeth Mayes. Sur. John Mayes. Wit. to bond, Sam'l Cobbs and Thos. Nash. p. S-1

18 September 1741. SPENCER, Thomas and Elizabeth J. Flournoy. Sur. John Nash. p. S-1

23 February 1758. STARK, Robert and Mary Hall, spinster. Sur. Thomas Claiborne. p. S-1

12 September 1811. St CLAIR, Archer and Sally Gibbs, who writes her consent to Arch^d St Clair. Wit. to consent, Thomas Gibbs and John Gibbs. Sur. Thomas Gibbs, who testifies Sally is 21. p. S-4

28 July 1808. St CLAIR, John and Betsy L. Hudson. Sur. George Walker and Parham Booker. p. S-3

20 May 1797. STEGER, Thomas and Elizabeth Goode, who writes her own consent, wit. by Garland Goode. Sur. Waller Ford. p. S-3

9 January 1765. STERN, Francis and Elizabeth Jones. Sur. Thos. Jones. p. S-1

19 October 1786. STILL, Jeremiah and Sally Wynne, dau. of John Wynne, who consents. Wit. to consent, John Bach and James Amos. Sur. Charles Featherston. Wit. to bond, James Townes, Jr. and Vivion Brooking. p. S-2

25 December 1756. STITH, Richard and Lucy Holt. Sur. David Holt. p. S-1

27 January 1764. STOKER, Robt., Junr. and Mary Dawson. Sur. John Winn. p. S-1

30 August 1799. STOKES, Allen and Elizabeth Green, dau. of Abraham Green, who consents. Wit. to consent, James Clark and John Hamlin. Sur. James Cocke. p. S-4

2 July 1760. STOKES, William and Lucretia Ellis, spinster, dau. of Thomas Ellis, who consents. Wit. to consent, John Barnes and Ellison Ellis. Sur. Ellison Ellis. p. S-1

14 April 1786. STOKES, William and Nancy Crenshaw. Sur. William Crenshaw. p. S-2

21 July 1801. STONE, Anderson and Patsy Ligon, dau. of Wm. Ligon, who consents. Wit. to consent, Woodson Ligon and Thomas Ligon. Sur. Thomas Ligon. Married 22 July by Rev. John Pollard. p. S-3

4 September 1795. STOTT, James and Edith Foster. Sur. J. Pollard Foster. p. S-3

28 January 1762. STOVALL, Bartholomew and Sally Brackett. Sur. Thomas Brackett. p. S-1

25 December 1793. STOW, Herbert and Susanah Cousins, who writes her own consent. Wit. to consent, William Adams, who is surety. p. S-3

16 February 1786. STOW, Jacob and Nancy Foard, dau. of George Ford, who consents. Wit. to consent, Arthur Leath and Alb--- Lewis. Sur. Richard Featherston. p. S-2

31 October 1806. STOW, William and Nancy Belcher, who writes her own consent, witnessed by Jesse Waldrope. Sur. Francis Belcher. p. S-3

6 October 1806. STRINGER, James and Winifred Dunnavant. Sur. Philip Dunnavant. Married 9 October by Rev. T. G. Leigh. p. S-3
(This marriage is listed twice in returns and Minister says Winnefred Dunnavant.)

4 December 1784. STURDEVANT, Daniel and Martha Perham,
dau. of William Perham, who consents. Sur. Henry Smith.
p. S-2 (Is this Parham?)

1 June 1805. SUBLETT, Peter D. and Nancy Wingo, dau. of
John Wingo, who consents. Wit. to consent, Dudley Seay
and Archibald Wingo. Sur. Dudley Seay. Married 1 June
by Rev. John Skurrey. p. S-3

24 April 1788. SUBLETT, William and Betsy Hughes. Sur.
John Hughes. p. S-2

29 July 1784. SUDBERRY, William and Frances Dunnavant,
who writes her own consent, wit. by John Wyley and Clark
Hort--? Sur. Samuel Booker. p. S-2

31 August 1767. SUGGITT, Edgcomb and Constance Edmundson,
both of Nottoway Parish. Constance is daughter of Upton
Edmondson, who consents. Wit. to consent, G. Lewis and
Bert Edmunson. Sur. Griffin Lewis. p. S-1
(Will of Upton Edmondson, W. B. 2, p. 9 names, among
others, wife Mary and "daughter Constance, wife of Edgcomb Suggett.")

20 January 1762. SULLIVANT, John and Sarah Seay, dau. of
Jacob Seay, who consents. Sur. John Seay. p. S-1
On 14 January, William Ford wrote the Court "to grant
John Sullivant license to marry." This is witnessed by
Jacob Seay and John Seay.

22 December 1763. TABB, Edward and Jean Clements. Sur.
Thomas Tabb. p. T-1

1 October 1765. TABB, John and Mary Mallory, of Nottoway Parish. Sur. Thomas Lowry. p. T-1

15 December 1784. TABB, John and Nancy Anderson, dau. of
Elizabeth Anderson, who consents. Wit. to consent,
Joseph Seay and Parham Anderson. Sur. Joseph Hillsman.
p. T-1

27 September 1735. TABB, Thomas and Rebecca Booker,
whose Guardian is John Hill. Sur. Richard Booker. p. T-1

18 October 1814. TABB, Thomas and Mary T. Bolling, who
writes her own consent, witnessed by William Old. Sur.
John R. Archer. p. T-3

19 May 1792. TALLEY, Abner and Elizabeth Powell. Jno.
Powell consents. Sur. Abram Powell. p. T-2

2 August 1811. TALLEY, Daniel and Nancy Galliway. Sur. Joseph Waltrip. Bidley Patton and David Tally testify that Daniel was 21 on 6 July 1811. p. T-3

24 April 1790. TALLEY, Grief and Ann Cousins, dau. of John Cousins, who consents. Wit. to consent, Thos. Vernon Brooking. Sur. Robert Crowder. Married 27 April by Rev. Robert Marshall, who says Capt. Grief Talley, Planter. p. T-2

21 April 1792. TALLEY, John and Jane Crowder. Sur. Joshua Spain. Married 21 May by Rev. Walthall Robertson. p. T-3

5 April 1808. TALLEY, John and Polly Pitchford, who writes her own consent, witnessed by Jesse Waltrip. Sur. John Pitchford. p. T-2

25 December 1781. TALLEY, Lodwick and Mary Talley. Consent of Daniel Coleman and Mary Talley, 24 December 1781, says Molley. Sur. William Old. p. T-1

2 September 1786. TALLEY, Peyton and Ridley Claiborne Powell. Sur. Robert Powell. p. T-1

28 September 1815. TALLEY, Woodley and Holly P. Hood. Sur. Laban Pitchford. NOTE on back of bond: "Laban Pitchford is son of Holly P. Hood." Married by Rev. James Chappell. p. T-3

2 January 1764. TANNER, Branch and Mary Page Finney. Sur. Josiah Tatum. p. T-1

2 June 1810. TANNER, Edward and Martha Powell, who writes her own consent, witnessed by Henry H. Southall, Jesse Southall and Nancy Southall. Sur. Jesse Southall, who testifies Martha is 21. Married 2 June by Rev. James Chappell. p. T-3

24 May 1804. TANNER, Elam and Mary Cliburn, dau. of Leonard Cliburn, who consents. Wit. to consent, Henry Southall and James Southall. Sur. Henry H. Southall. p. T-2   (Claiborne?)

27 May 1813. TANNER, Field and Lucy Hastings, whose consent is dated 25 May 1813. Wit. to consent, Henry H. Southall and Robert Tanner. Henry Southall testifies Lucy is 21. Sur. Henry H. Southall. p. T-3

5 May 1764. TANNER, Lodwick and Ann Johnson, widow. Sur. Richard Hayes. p. T-1

16 February 1810. TANNER, William and Betsey Powell. On
16 February Grief B. Powell testifies Betsey is 21. Sur.
Grief B. Hawkins. Married 16 February by Rev. James Chappell. p. T-3

3 May 1779. TATUM, Henry and Sally Scott, dau. of John
Scott, deceased. Her Guardian, George Carrington, consents for her. Sur. John Walthall. p. T-1

21 December 1791. TATUM, Zachariah and Judith Walker,
dau. of Edmund Walker, who consents. Wit. to consent,
George Walker. Sur. Henry Tatum. p. T-2

5 September 1766. TAYLOR, James and Martha Booker,
widow. Sur. John Smith. p. T-1

4 February 1805. TAYLOR, James D. and Judith Vasser.
Consent of Judith Vasser is dated 4 February 1805. Wit.
to consent, William Vasser, who is surety. p. T-2
(NOTE: The Register says 6 February - bond and consent
say 4 February.)

27 November 1784. THOMAS, David and Martha Hurt. Sur.
William Meanly. p. T-1

22 March 1781. THOMAS, Joshua and Patty Chappell. Moses
Hurt, Sr., Guardian to Patty, consents. Consent dated
21 March 1781. Wit. to consent, Lee Cocke and Nancy
Hurt. Sur. Richard Locke. p. T-1

18 December 1788. THOMAS, Woodlif and Sarah Williams,
who writes her own consent. Wit. to consent, Arthur
Scott, Peleg Farguson and Jno. Farguson. Sur. Arthur
Scott. p. T-2

4 September 1781. THOMPSON, John and Agnes Brogan (?).
Married by Rev. Jeremiah Walker. Minister's Return.

1 November 1804. THOMPSON, John and Sally Crawley
Jones, dau. of John Jones, whose consent says John Thompson is of Dinwiddie County. Wit. to consent, Jos: Moore
and David Jones. Sur. David C. Jones. p. T-2

8 November 1788. THOMPSON, Josiah and Christian Ford,
dau. of Mary Ford, who consents. Wit. to consent, Richard Anderson and Mary Anderson. Sur. Reinard Anderson.
p. T-2

11 December 1788. THOMPSON, Randolph and Mary Wilkerson,
who writes her own consent. Wit. to consent, James Tom-
son. Sur. Wm. Daniels. p. T-2

18 December 1756. THOMPSON, Richard and Jemima Cabiness.
Sur. T. Claiborne. William Westbrook consents. Wit. to
consent, John White and Joseph White. p. T-1

3 March 1792. THOMPSON, Thomas and Ann Allen, who writes
her own consent. Sur. Bryant Butler. Married 6 March by
Rev. Walter G. Robertson. p. T-3

21 September 1804. THOMPSON, William B. and Prudence
Mann, dau. of Field Mann, who consents. Wit. to consent, David Mann and he is surety. p. T-2

2 May 1750. THOMSON, Roger and Ann Farguson. John Farguson consents. Sur. Jeremiah Keen. p. T-1

26 October 1785. THOMSON, Washington and Jean Stott,
dau. of James Stott, who consents. Wit. to consent,
Eleazer Clay and Christopher Robertson. Sur. James Farley. Married by Rev. Simeon Walton. p. T-1

25 November 1812. THOMSON, Wilson and Polley Wright.
Married by Rev. John Pollard. Minister's Return.

6 March 1784. THORNTON, Reuben and Prudence Munford.
Freeman Munford consents. Consent dated 5 February 1784.
Wit. to consent, John Gooch, and he is surety. p. T-1

12 February 1777. THORNTON, Sterling Clack and Mary
Jones, widow. Sur. Robert Foster. p. T-1

19 November 1777. THORP, William and Mary Farley, dau.
of Stewart Farley, whose consent is witnessed by Keziah
Farley and F---- Thorp. Sur. Nathaniel Farley. p. T-1

24 August 1809. THURSTON, James H. and Sally R. Mottley,
whose Guardian, George Baldwin, consents. Wit. to consent, Booker Foster. Sur. Henry Thurston and Booker Foster. Married 25 August by Rev. John Pollard, Senr.
p. T-2

9 November 1802. TIBBS, James and Agnes Anian, who
writes her own consent. Wit. to consent, George Anian,
who is surety. Married 10 November by Rev. William
Dier. p. T-3

19 January 1782. TIMBERLAKE, John and Elizabeth Pryor,
dau. of John Pryor, who consents. Sur. Sterling C. Thornton. p. T-1

13 January 1779. TOMS, Edward and Elizabeth Ford, dau. of
Mary Ford who consents. Sur. Henry Walthall. p. T-1
(NOTE: Edward's name has been given as Towns and Tomes - he
signs Edwd Toms and consent says Edw. Toms. K.B.W.)

5 February 1800. TOWNES, Armistead T. and Rebecca H.
Booker. Sur. James Townes, Jr. p. T-2

30 November 1808. TOWNES, A. T. and Elizabeth Moseley
Giles. John Royster, Elizabeth's Guardian, requests this
license. Request dated 22 October 1808, witnessed by John
Hobday. Sur. Bentley Anderson. p. T-2

29 September 1792. TOWNES, James and Rachel M. Booker.
Sur. Charles Burch. Married by Rev. John Brunskill, who
says Rachel Marrott Booker. p. T-3

22 December 1806. TOWNES, John L., Jr. and Polly Segar
Eggleston, whose Guardian, Joseph Eggleston, consents.
Sur. John Townes, Sr. p. T-2

11 December 1786. TRABUE, Joseph and Mary Ann Hughes.
Sur. John Hughes. p. T-1

19 July 1803. TRAYLOR, Archibald and Judith Webster,
dau. of Anthony Webster, Sr., who consents. Wit. to consent, Thomas Taylor and Anthony Webster. Sur. Edward
Webster. p. T-2

23 May 1805. TRENT, William and Mary Ann Franklin Leneve
(LeNeve?), who writes her own consent. Wit. to consent,
Parham Booker and Francis Pride. Sur. Mathew Moseley.
Married by Rev. John Skurrey. p. T-2
(NOTE: The Register says Mary Ann Franklin League - bond
and consent say Mary Ann Franklin Leneve.)

28 May 1784. TRUIT, William and Elizabeth Brown. Sur.
John Farley. p. T-1

8 December 1810. TUCKER, Absalom and Polly Tucker. Abel
Tucker consents and he is surety. Wit. to consent, Abel
Tucker, Senr. p. T-3

12 October 1797. TUCKER, Benjamin and Jency Spinner,
dau. of Jency Spinner, whose consent says, "my daughter, Jency." Wit. to consent, Thomas Harman and Abel
Mann. Sur. Abel Mann. p. T-2

23 December 1809. TUCKER, Boswell and Judith Elam. Sur.
Abram Powell. Married 23 December by Rev. James Chappell.
p. T-2

4 February 1782. TUCKER, David and Fanny Old. Sur.
Robert Tucker. p. T-1

4 August 1784. TUCKER, Francis and Martha Huddleston.
Sur. Robert Crowder. p. T-1

6 March 1787. TUCKER, Henry and Elizabeth Murry, who writes her own consent. Wit. to consent, Thos. Jackson and Wm. Jackson. Sur. Field Tanner. p. T-2

2 March 1793. TUCKER, Henry and Mary Maury, dau. of Elizabeth Tucker, who consents. Wit. to consent, Abraham Burton and John Martin. Sur. Abram Burton. p. T-2

14 March 1787. TUCKER, Hezekiah and Amy Tucker. Henry Tucker consents. Wit. to consent, Samuel Chappell and Ster. C. Thornton. Sur. Sterling C. Thornton. p. T-1

25 November 1788. TUCKER, Joel and Elizabeth Clements, who signs her consent, Elizabeth Clemons. Wit. to consent, John Clemons and Anna Clemons. Sur. John Clemons. p. T-2

26 February 1779. TUCKER, Joseph and Ann Sallard, dau. of Charles Sallard, who consents. Sur. Zachariah Hurt. Joseph Tucker is of Dinwiddie County. p. T-1

17 March 1788. TUCKER, Mathew and Elizabeth Rease. Sur. Is. Holmes. p. T-2   (Isaac Holmes is in top of bond.)

24 April 1799. TUCKER, Nelson and Rhoda Hood. Sur. Solomon Hood. Married 2 May by Rev. Walthall Robertson. p. T-2

22 December 1787. TUCKER, Paschal and Tabitha Eckles, dau. of Thomas Eckles, who consents. Sur. Edward Eckles. p. T-2
(Was this a double wedding? See Edward Eckles.)

7 December 1778. TUCKER, Robert and Mary Hawks. Sur. Daniel Tucker. p. T-1

23 January 1793. TUCKER, Thomas and Mary Coleman, who writes her own consent. Wit. to consent, Benjamin Woodback (?). Sur. Evan Mitchell. Married 28 January by Rev. Robert Walthall, who says: Thomas Tucker, Planter. p. T-2

13 August 1800. TUCKER, Thomas and Elizabeth Coleman. Sur. Martin Chandler. Married 16 August by Rev. Walthall Robertson. p. T-2

7 October 1791. TUCKER, Thompson and Clarresy Murray. Sur. Thomas Murray. p. T-2   SEE Thompson Tucker.

10 November 1791. TUCKER, Thompson and Charity Murry. Married by Rev. Robert Walthall, who says, Thompson Tucker, Planter. Minister's Return. SEE Thompson Tucker.

26 October 1756. TUCKER, William and Mary Keats. Curtis
Keats' request for this license says, "My daughter." Wit.
to request, Robert Tucker. Sur. Robert Tucker, Jr.
p. T-1

22 June 1810. TUCKER, William and Sally Tucker. Abel
Tucker consents and he is surety. Wit. to consent, Abso-
lom Tucker and Absolom Tucker, Jr. Married 23 June by
Rev. James Chappell. p. T-3

18 June 1781. TYE, Solomon and Sally Bates. Sur.
Younger Hardwick, of Dinwiddie County. p. T-1
(NOTE: The Register says Lucy Bates - the bond says
Sally Bates.)

5 March 1768. VADEN, Henry and Susanna Green. Sur.
Abraham Green. p. V-1

17 March 1783. VADEN, Henry and Judith Hawks, who writes
her own consent. Sur. _____ _____. p. V-1

13 November 1785. VADEN, Herod and Susannah Smith, who
writes her own consent. Wit. to consent, Grief Talley
and Sherwood Smith. Sur. Grief Talley. Married 21
November by Rev. Devereux Jarratt. p. V-1

27 January 1778. VASSA, William and Elizabeth Jackson.
Sur. Ro. Lawson. p. V-1   (Should this be Vasser?)

10 January 1789. VASSER, Daniel and Frances Anderson.
Sur. John Anderson. p. V-1

1 February 1781. VASSER, Richard and Frances Shalteen
(?). Wit. to her consent, Anthony Webster, who is
surety. p. V-1

26 January 1804. VERSER, William and Mary Webster, who
says William Vasser in her consent. Sur. William Warriner. Married 24 February by Rev. Samuel Rucker, who says
William Vasser. p. V-1

7 November 1803. VAUGHAN, Asa and Jane Truly, dau. of
John Truly, Senr., whose consent is dated 7 November
1803. Sur. Grief Truly. p. V-1

22 December 1800. VAUGHAN, Craddock and Elizabeth Clough.
Sur. Allen Townes. Married by Rev. David Thomson. p. V-1

27 November 1794. VAUGHAN, Francis and Magdeline Walker.
James Vaughan, Jr., her Guardian, consents. Wit. to consent, Claiborn Anderson and John Booth. Sur. James Craddock. p. V-1

-- October 1791. VAUGHAN, James and Frances Jackson, dau. of Francis Jackson, who consents. Consent dated 26 October 1791. Wit. to consent, Chas. Craddock and Standley Chaffin. Sur. Richard Clough. p. V-1

29 December 1791. VAUGHAN, James and Mary Clough. Sur. Richard Clough. p. V-1

28 July 1792. VAUGHAN, James and Martha Legg. Sur. John Morris. p. V-1

22 February 1810. VAUGHAN, James and Jane H. Craddock, whose Guardian, Robert Vaughan, is surety. Married 23 February by Rev. John Pollard, Senr. p. V-1

25 May 1757. VAUGHAN, John and Elizabeth Stanley, widow, who writes her own consent. Wit. to consent, Caleb Perkinson and Windy Waller. Sur. Daniel Murray. p. V-1

21 November 1759. VAUGHAN, John and Jane Worsham, widow, who writes her own consent. Sur. Thomas Bottom. p. V-1

8 February 1786. VAUGHAN, John and Martha Williams, dau. of Philip Williams, Senr., who consents. Wit. to consent, Abraham Forrest and Philip Williams, Junr. Sur. Philip Williams, Junr. p. V-1

20 February 1790. VAUGHAN, John and Sarah Walker, whose consent is witnessed by William Gill and Thos. Smith. Sur. Patrick Vaughan. p. V-1

26 March 1788. VAUGHAN, Lewis and Sally Davenport, who writes her own consent, witnessed by Geo. Davenport and Susanner Featherston. Sur. Burwell Featherston. Married by Rev. Charles Anderson. p. V-1

2 October 1811. VAUGHAN, Milton and Rebecca C. Craddock, who "gives her own consent." Sur. Wm. Leigh. Married 3 October by Rev. Zachariah G. Leigh. p. V-1

20 January 1799. VAUGHAN, Robert and Sarah Craddock, "widow and relict of William Craddock, deceased, of this County." Sur. John Truly. p. V-1

22 April 1810. VAUGHAN, Thomas and Tallitha Howell. Sur. Benj. Wynn. p. V-1

17 March 1813. VAUGHAN, William H. and Martha Chappell. John Chappell's consent is witnessed by Milton Vaughan and Sam¹ Overton. Sur. Samuel Overton. Married 17 March by Rev. Zachariah G. Leigh. p. V-1

7 February 1778. VAUGHAN, Willis and Edith Gunn. James
Gunn consents. Wit. to his consent, Alexander Roberts and
James Vaughan. Sur. Alexander Roberts. p. V-1

16 December 1796. VAUGHAN, Willis and Betsy Wright, dau.
of Thomas Wright, Senr., who consents. Wit. to consent,
Reuben Wright and Pleasant Wright. Sur. Reuben Wright.
p. V-1

22 December 1807. VEST, Samuel and Betsy W. Johnson,
whose Guardian, William Johnson, consents. Consent dated
19 December 1807. Wit. to consent, David Johnson and
John Carter. Sur. John Carter. p. V-1

27 November 1788. WADDELL, Jacob and Drucilla League,
dau. of James League, whose consent is witnessed by,
Nathaniel Waddill and Beverly Fleming. Sur. Beverly
Fleming. p. W-3

23 June 1806. WADDELL, Miller and Nancy Harper, whose
Guardian, Thompson Scott, consents. Sur. James Craddock.
Married 26 June by Rev. John Pollard. p. W-5-a

31 August 1795. WALD, Burwell and Prudence Coleman, who
writes her own consent, dated 31 August 1795. Wit. to
consent, William Adams and David A. Barnes. Sur. Laban
Coleman. p. W-5-a

9 September 1807. WALDEN, Samuel and Sally Carpenter.
Bentley Anderson and Joel Belcher testify Sally is of
age. Sur. Joel Belcher. Married 10 September by Rev.
William Dier. p. W-4

4 November 1789. WALKE, John and Hannah Finney, who
writes her own consent. Wit. to consent, Thos: Brooking.
Sur. James Robertson. p. W-4

22 December 1757. WALKER, Alex^r and Frances Scott, spinster. Robert Jones requests this license on 22 December
1757. Wit. to request, Sam Jones and John Scott, Junr.
Sur. Edmund Walker. p. W-1

28 April 1768. WALKER, Ben and Sarah Hudson, dau. of
Thos. Hudson, who consents. Sur. Mackness Goode, of
Prince Edward County. Ben is son of Benjamin Walker, of
Prince Edward County, who consents. p. W-1

9 September 1794. WALKER, James and Nancy Mayes, dau. of
Daniel Mayes, who consents. Sur. Francis Jones. Married
10 September by Rev. Walthall Robertson. p. W-5-a

Since October 1787. WALKER, John and Eliz^a Trotter.
Married by Rev. Charles Anderson. Minister's Return.

16 November 1781. WALKER, William T. and Frances Williamson. Jacob Williamson consents. Sur. Hopkins Muse.
p. W-2

12 November 1812. WALLACE, Samuel and Elizabeth Asselin.
Her Guardian, John Jeter consents. Wit. to consent,
Sterling Ford and Reuben Wright. Sur. Sterling Ford.
Married by Rev. John Pollard. p. W-5-b

17 February 1791. WALTHALL, Bartley and Ann Purkinson,
who writes her own consent. Wit. to consent, Richard
Walthall, who is surety. Married 24 February by Rev.
Robert Walthall, who says Bartley Walthall, Carpenter.
p. W-4

6 April 1796. WALTHALL, Christopher and Sally Sudberry.
Sur. John Sudberry. p. W-5-b

22 February 1791. WALTHALL, Henry and Elizabeth Ends,
dau. of Henry Ends, whose consent is dated 20 February,
and he signs: Henry Ends. Wit. to consent, Bartley
Baugh and John Marshall. Sur. John Clemons. p. W-4
(Should this name be Eanes?)

3 January 1782. WALTHALL, John and Grace Booker. Sur.
Wm. M. Booker. p. W-2

20 December 1777. WALTHALL, Robert and Lucy Walthall,
dau. of Thomas Walthall, who consents. Sur. William Walthall, Senr. p. W-2

6 April 1752. WALTHALL, William and Anna Elam, spinster.
Robert Elam, Senr. consents. Wit. to consent, Thomas
Stratton and Mary Elam. Sur. Christopher Walthall.
p. W-1

18 February 1775. WALTHALL, William, Junr. and Lucy
Willson, both of Raleigh Parish. Sur. John Willson,
Senr. p. W-1

7 June 1781. WALTHALL, William and Sally Perkinson.
Sur. William Old. p. W-2

17 November 1795. WALTHALL, William and Nancy Walthall.
Lucy Walthall consents. Wit. to consent, Bartley Walthall and Peter Walthall. Sur. Bartley Walthall.
p. W-5-b

17 May 1787. WALTON, John and Susanna Anderson, dau. of
Charles Anderson, who consents. Wit. to consent, Larkin
Anderson and Simeon Walton. Sur. Mathew Anderson. Mar-
ied by Rev. Charles Anderson. p. W-3

16 July 1788. WALTON, John and Mary Jenkins, dau. of
James Jenkins, who consents. Wit. to consent, Sher. Walton and Mathew Walton. Sur. Mathew Walton. p. W-3

1 March 1809. WALTON, Thomas H. and Ann H. Hatcher,
widow, dau. of Ludd^W Brackett, who consents. Sur. Wilson
Brackett. p. W-5-b

1 August 1809. WALTRIP, Jesse and Polly Galloway, who
writes her own consent. Wit. to consent, Spencer Perrin,
who is surety. p. W-5-b

9 March 1792. WALTRIP, Joseph and Polly McCann. Sur.
John McCann. p. W-5-b

13 January 1779. WARD, Benjamin and Mary Eggleston, dau.
of Joseph Eggleston, who consents. Sur. Stith Hardaway.
Benjamin Ward is of Chesterfield County. p. W-2

15 April 1786. WARD, Claiborne and Nancy Butler, dau. of
William Butler, who consents. Wit. to consent, Samuel
Jones and John Jones. Sur. John Jones. p. W-3

20 December 1792. WARD, Edward and Ann Jones, dau. of
William Jones, whose consent, dated 18 December 1792, says:
"Edward Ward to marry my daughter Ann on the 25th of this
month." Sur. Edward Wilkinson. p. W-5-a

25 October 1746. WARD, Henry and Prudence Jones, dau. of
Richard Jones, who consents. Sur. Henry Anderson. p. W-1

30 March 1789. WARD, John and Dosey Anderson, dau. of
Henry Anderson, who consents. Wit. to consent, James
Jennings, Henry Jennings and Blackman Ward. Sur. Daniel
Beasley. p. W-4

24 January 1748. WARD, Joseph and Martha Burton. Sur.
John Burton. p. W-1

7 June 1786. WARD, Levy and Susannah Clarke. Sur. Henry
Jones. p. W-3

26 February 1801. WARD, Peter and Martha (No name here).
Sur. Edward Ward. This bond is not in the Register.

10 November 1752. WARD, Rowland and _____ce Jones,
spinster, dau. of Richard Jones. Sur. James Claiborne.
p. W-1

7 April 1777. Ward, Rowland, Junr. and Sarah Ward, both of Raleigh Parish. Edm^d Ward, her Guardian, consents. Wit. to consent, Saml Booker and Davis Booker. Sur. Francis Anderson. p. W-2

10 February 1778. WARD, Wiley and Ann Thomas, of Nottoway Parish, who writes her own consent. Wit. to consent, William Thomas and John Worsham. Sur. John Worsham. p. W-2

28 February 1784. WARD, Wiley and Sally Ford. Sur. John Wynne. p. W-2

23 June 1787. WARD, Wiley and Martha Mayes. Sur. William Gates. p. W-3

20 October 1804. WARD, William and Sarah Jones. Chamberlain Jones' consent says William C. Ward. Wit. to consent, Polly B. Anderson and Benjamin B. Jones. Sur. Benjamin Jones. p. W-5-a

18 December 1805. WARD, William, Jr. and Sally W. Elmore, dau. of Thos. Elmore, who is surety. p. W-5-a

28 August 1788. WARE, Thomas and Sarah Wingo, dau. of John Wingo, who consents. Wit. to consent, John Wingo and Churchill Wingo. Sur. D. Cashon. (Up in the bond his name is written David Cashon.) p. W-3

28 January 1803. WARRINER, William and Karen H. Dunnavant, who writes her own consent. Wit. to consent, T. Dunnavant. Sur. Samuel Dunnavant. p. W-5-b

5 February 1781. WASHINGTON, Geo. and Lucy Greenhill. Thos. Williams, her Guardian, consents. Wit. to consent, Isaac Jackson and Philip W. Greenhill. Sur. Samuel Greenhill. p. W-2

18 November 1814. WATERS, John and Polly Tucker, dau. of Benjamin Tucker, who testifies John Waters is of age, and he is surety. Married 20 November by Rev. James Chappell. p. W-5-b

27 October 1791. WATERS, William and Sarah Barding. Her mother, Rachel Bass, consents. Wit. to consent, J. Wil--- and W. Ford. Sur. Henry Clayton. p. W-4

26 February 1779. WATKINS, James and Jane Thompson. Sur. Wm. Thompson. James Watkins is of Charlotte County. p. W-2

15 J--y 1752. WATKINS, Joel and Rhody Gresham, dau. of Barbary Gresham, who consents. Sur. John Pride. p. W-1

16 November 1787. WATKINS, Samuel and Eleanor Thompson, dau. of Drury Thompson, who consents. Wit. to consent, James Watkins, Junr. and Daniel Marshall. Sur. Daniel Marshall. Married by Rev. S. Walton. p. W-3

28 November 1775. WATKINS, Thomas and Magdalene Dupuy, dau. of John B. Dupuy. Sur. Jno. Bouth Dupuy. p. W-1

16 March 1804. WATSON, Benjamin and Mary Willson. Sur. Richard M. Jones. p. W-4

7 December 1763. WATSON, John and Mary Smith, spinster. Sur. George Smith. p. W-1

23 September 1739. WATSON, William and Amy Jones. Sur. Samuel Tarry. p. W-1   (The bond is mutilated.)

11 June 1794. WEATHERFORD, William and Jane Chapman, · dau. of John Chapman, Sr., whose consent says, "My daughter, Jane." Wit. to consent, Benjamin Chapman and William Chapman. Sur. Joel Compton. Married 11 June by Rev. James McGlasson, who says Jean. p. W-5-a

19 February 1786. WEBBER, Seth and Sally White Chapman, dau. of John Chapman, Sr., who consents. Wit. to consent, Richd Webber and Wm. Chapman. Sur. Richard Webber. p. W-3

30 January 1798. WEBSTER, Anthony and Polly C. Foster, dau. of Booker Foster, who consents. Wit. to consent, Jarratt Rison and Wm. Webster. Sur. William Webster. p. W-4

8 December 1809. WEBSTER, Archibald and Nancy Ellison Ellmore, who writes her own consent. Wit. to consent, Thos: Elmore, Wm. Ward and Thomas W. Webster. Sur. Thos: W. Webster. Married 17 December by Rev. Joseph Finnell, who says Nancy Ellison Ellmore. p. W-5-b
(NOTE: The Register says Nancy Ellington Elmore - bond, consent and Minister's return say Nancy Ellison Ellmore.)

22 December 1797. WEBSTER, Edward and Elizabeth Crowder, dau. of William Crowder, who consents. Wit. to consent, Allen Jeter and John Baldwin. Sur. John Baldwin. p. W-5-a

26 November 1792. WEBSTER, James and Anne Rison, who writes her own consent, Sur. Ellery Rison. p. W-4
SEE: John Webster.

2 April 1787. WEBSTER, John and Tabitha Robertson. Sur. Thomas Dier. p. W-3

Since 15 January 1791. WEBSTER, John and Elizabeth
Rison. Married by Rev. John Brunskill. Minister's
Return. SEE: James Webster.

23 December 1793. WEBSTER, John and Clarisy Smithey,
dau. of Joshua Smithey, who consents. Wit. to consent,
Thomas Webster and William Webster. Sur. Thomas Webster.
p. W-5-a

27 August 1807. WEBSTER, John, Jr. and Mary H. Webster,
who writes her own consent. Wit. to consent, Abel Webster, who is surety. p. W-5-a

30 October 1804. WEBSTER, Miles and Rebecca Webster, who
writes her own consent. Wit. to consent, John Webster, Jr.
Sur. Thos: Rowlett. p. W-5-a

27 October 1761. WEBSTER, Peter, Jr. and Elizabeth Gibbs,
dau. of Mary Gibbs, who consents. Wit. to consent, Dib[ll]
Holt and William Gibbs. Sur. Thomas Webster. p. W-1

27 August 1795. WEBSTER, Peter and Kezza Crittenden, who
writes her own consent as Cizey. Wit. to consent, John
Crittenden and Anthony Webster. Sur. John Crittenden.
p. W-5-b

14 December 1796. WEBSTER, Peter, Jr. and Mary Hill
Johnson. Sur. James Johnson. p. W-5-a

11 October 1762. WEBSTER, Thomas and Ann Brooks. Sur.
Thomas Brooks. p. W-1

30 November 1795. WEBSTER, William and Bell Wright Fos-
ter, dau. of Booker Foster, whose consent says Betsy.
Wit. to consent, Thomas W. McGlasson and James McGlasson.
Sur. Thomas McGlasson. Married 9 December by Rev. James
McGlasson, who says Eliza Wright Foster. p. W-5-b

9 May 1795. WEEKS, Richard and Judith Willson. Mary
Wilson consents. Wit. to consent, Jesse Reese, who is
surety. p. W-4

17 March 1781. WEEKS, William and Ann Bennitt. Sur.
Robert French. p. W-2

15 December 1764. WEST, Abraham and Philadelphia Lawson. Her Guardian, David Greenhill, consents. Wit. to
consent, John Mackie, John Phillips and Henry Dennis.
Sur. Richard Dennis. p. W-1

20 April 1803. WEST, Henry and Patsy Reinhard, dau. of Martha Reinhard, who consents for "daughter Patsy" on 19 April 1803. Wit. to consent, James Worsham and Thomas Worsham. Sur. Walter Ford. Married 21 April by Rev. John Skurrey. p. W-5-b   (Walter or Waller? Ford.)

14 November 1798. WHITE, Caleb and Ann Seay, who writes her own consent. Sur. James Hillsman. p. W-4

28 January 1768. WHITE, John and Anna Clements, widow of Wm. Clements, Junr. Sur. Edward Tabb. p. W-1

7 October 1783. WHITE, Matthew and Martha Hayes. Sur. Richard Hayes. p. W-2

27 December 1784. WHITE, Richard and Jenny Compton, dau. of Elizabeth Compton, who consents. Sur. John White. p. W-3

12 May 1815. WHITE, Willis and Martha W. Clayborne, dau. of Wm. Clayborne, who consents. Wit. to consent, John White and Ann E. Pope. Sur. John White. Married 15 May by Rev. John Skurrey. p. W-6

18 January 1813. WHITWORTH, Jacob and Mary Allen. Samuel Allen consents. Wit. to consent, James Allen and A. Pride. Sur. Anderson Pride. Married 21 January by Rev. John Skurrey. p. W-5-b

21 January 1790. WHITWORTH, Roland and Martha Walthall, dau. of Daniel Walthall, who consents. Wit. to consent, John Ellis and William Ellis. Sur. Claiborne Whitworth. p. W-4

11 June 1788. WILKERSON, Anthony and Elizabeth Ellington, who writes her own consent. Wit. to consent, Henry Furgusson and Sarah Furgusson. Sur. Henry Furgusson. Married by Rev. Charles Anderson. p. W-3

1 December 1787. WILKES, Burwell and Elizabeth Gunn. James and Elizabeth Gunn consent. Wit. to consent, William Gunn and Elijah Gunn. Sur. William Gunn. Married 3 December by Rev. John King. p. W-3

29 January 1759. WILKERSON, Edward and Mary Oglesby, widow. Sur. William Archer. Edward Wilkerson is of Chesterfield County. p. W-1

2 July 1782. WILKINSON, Daniel and Ann Powell. Sur. Robert Powell. p. W-2

28 Feby. 1788. WILKINSON, Joseph and Obedience Branch.
Her Guardian, Benjamin Branch, consents. Wit. to consent,
Edward Bass and T. Perkinson. Sur. Thomas Jones. p. W-3

26 January 1758. WILKINSON, Nathaniel and Elizabeth Willson, spinster. Sur. Daniel Willson. p. W-1

5 March 1784. WILKINSON, Stephen and Tabitha Morgan.
Sur. John Morgan. p. W-3

31 July 1793. WILKINSON, William and Lucy Moseley. Sur.
Geo. Rowlett. p. W-5-a

24 November 1785. WILLIAMS, James and Jamima Gunn, who
writes her own consent. Her father, James Gunn, certifies his consent. Sur. George Hightower. p. W-3

9 June 1797. WILLIAMS, James and Lucy _____, dau. of
Geo. _____. Sur. James Townes, Jr. p. W-5-b
(This bond is mutilated.)

16 March 1759. WILLIAMS, John and Mary Atwood. James
Atwood consents. Wit. to consent, Dan Williams, Junr.
and George Forest. Sur. Richard Atwood. p. W-1

4 May 1785. WILLIAMS, Josiah and Judith Elmore. Sur.
Thos. Elmore. p. W-3

22 December 1801. WILLIAMS, Philip, Jr. and Elizabeth
Woodson. Joseph Woodson consents. Wit. to consent,
Isham League, who is surety. Married 24 December by
Rev. John Skurrey. p. W-4

17 December 1808. WILLIAMS, Philip, Jr. and Polly Mitchell. Sur. John Mitchell. Married 20 December by Rev.
John Skurrey. p. W-5-b

22 December 1766. WILLIAMS, Samuel and Susannah Ligon.
Sur. William Ligon. p. W-1
(NOTE: On the outside of this bond is 27 Dec. - on the
inside of the bond is 22 December.)

7 December 1803. WILLIAMS, Samuel and Betsy Wingo, dau.
of John Wingo whose consent is dated 7 December 1803.
Wit. to consent, Dudley Seay and Rachel Seay. Sur. Dudley Seay. Married 8 December by Rev. John Skurrey.
Returned 23 August 1804. p. W-5-b

25 January 1810. WILLIAMS, Samuel and Polly Noble, dau.
of John Noble, who consents. Wit. to consent, Elizabeth
Pollard. Sur. Robt. L. Smithey. Married 26 January by
Rev. John Pollard, Senr. p. W-5-b

13 August 1779. WILLIAMS, Sterling and Elizabeth Morgan.
Sur. Peter Ellington. p. W-2

20 December 1762. WILLIAMS, Thomas and Elizabeth Watson.
Sur. Richard Jones. p. W-1

25 November 1807. WILLIAMS, Thomas and Polley Baldwin.
Sur. George Baldwin. Married 10 December by Rev. John
Skurrey. p. W-4

11 July 1788. WILLIAMS, William and Mary Jordan. James
Jordan consents. Wit. to consent, Batte Cooke and Robert
Parrish. Sur. Phillip Greenhill. p. W-3

9 June 17--. WILLIAMSON, Benjamin and Amey Green. Sur.
Thos. Bevill. p. W-1   (This bond is mutilated.)

31 October 1769. WILLIAMSON, George and Ann Williamson,
dau. of Jacob Williamson, who is surety. p. W-1

25 February 1808. WILLIAMSON, Granville and Christiany
Foster. Sur. Booker Foster. p. W-5-a

16 December 1811. WILLIAMSON, Jacob and Mary W. Walker.
George Walker consents. Wit. to consent, Edmund B. Walker and Thomas W. Walker. Sur. W. T. Craddock. p. W-5-b

23 August 1764. WILLIAMSON, Lewellin and Sarah Lewis,
dau. of Geo. Lewis, whose consent says Lewelling Williamson. Wit. to consent, David Thweat and James Rees. Sur.
Lewellin Jones. p. W-1

13 July 1750. WILLIAMSON, William and Martha Green.
Sur. William Booker. p. W-1

24 May 1755. WILLS, Tilmer (Filmer?) and Elizabeth
Rebecca Green. Sur. Abraham Green. p. W-1

24 May 1810. WILLS, John and Lucy Newman. Sur. William
Walthall. p. W-5-b

19 December 1815. WILLS, John and Cary J. Clay. Sur.
Daniel W. Clay. Married 23 December by Rev. James Chappell. p. W-5-b

9 February 1815. WILLS, Lawrence and Judith B. Willson,
whose Guardian, Robert Tanner, consents. Wit. to consent,
Thomas Huddleston and John Tanner. Sur. Thomas Huddleston. Married 15 February by Rev. James Chappell. p. W-6

15March 1793. WILLS, Matthew and Lucy Walthall, whose consent is witnessed by Andrew Waugh and Edm[d] Wills, Sr. Sur.
Abra[m] Green. p. W-5-a

20 May 1795. WILLS, Matthew and Eliza Cousins, who writes her own consent. Wit. to consent, Grief Talley and James Worsham. Sur. James Worsham. p. W-5-b

13 June 1803. WILLS, Thomas and Polley Farley, dau. of Mathew Farley, who consents. Wit. to consent, Peter Farley and _____ Drake. Sur. Peter Farley. p. W-5-a

14 June 1774. WILLS, Thomas Tabb and Elizabeth Ridley Morgan, dau. of Samuel Morgan, who consents. Wit to consent, John Morgan, Simon Morgan and Charles Wilson. Sur. John Morgan. p. W-1

25 September 1811. WILLS, William and Ridley Branch, who writes her own consent, witnessed by Sam[l] Perry and Wood Jones, Jr. Sur. Wood Jones, Jr., who testifies Ridley is of age. p. W-5-b

WILLSON - WILSON

16 June 1780. WILSON, Chas. and Rachel Clarke, of Nottoway Parish. Sur. John Wilson. p. W-2

28 February 1776. WILLSON, Daniel, Jr. and Ann Finney. Sur. T. B. Willson. p. W-2

27 August 1789. WILLSON, Daniel and Elizabeth Anderson, dau. of Francis Anderson, who is surety. p. W-4

6 December 1794. WILLSON, James and Mary Cardwell, dau. of Richard Cardwell, who consents. Wit. to consent, Richard Weaks, who is surety. Married 11 December by Rev. Walthall Robertson. p. W-4

22 June 1758. WILLSON, John and Mary Israel. Sur. William Hall. William Wall gives consent for John Willson. Wit. to consent, T. Gilliam and Thomas Bottom. p. W-1

11 October 1792. WILSON, John and Lucy French, who writes her own consent. Sur. Thos. L. Wilson. p. W-4

2 May 1796. WILLSON, Peter and Patsy Tanner, dau. of Robert Tanner, who consents. Wit. to consent, William W. Hall, who is surety. p. W-5-a

28 February 1760. WILLSON, Tom Branch and Eliza: Finney. Robert Goode's consent says Elizabeth Finney, spinster. Wit. to consent, William Adams and George Ragsdale. Sur. Daniel Wilson. p. W-1

27 November 1777. WILLSON, Tom Branch and "Penefee" Barrat. Sur. John Booker. p. W-2

1 April 1782. WILLSON, Tom B. and Sarah Walthall. Sur.
John T. Peachy. p. W-2

15 August 1796. WILLSON, Thomas F. and Ann Anderson.
Sur. Daniel Willson. T. B. Willson consents for son,
Thomas Friend Willson. p. W-4

28 April 1769. WILLSON, William and Frances Cousins, of
Raleigh Parish. Sur. John Cousins. p. W-2

22 May 1782. WILY, John and Sally Mumford, dau. of Thomas Mumford, who consents. Sur. John C. Cobbs. p. W-2

26 November 1781. WINFREE, Robert and Susanna Crowder.
Consent for this marriage is signed: John Morgan, George
Worsham, Esqr., Mary Crowder and Susanna Crowder. Sur.
Robert Crowder. p. W-2

14 March 1810. WINFREY, Henry and Sally P. Totty, who
writes her own consent. Wit. to consent, Edward Totty
and Charles A. Cousins. Sur. Charles A. Cousins.
p. W-5-b
The following note was with Sally's consent.
"This is to certify that Mr. Winfrey, the bearer, quali-
fied at Dinwiddie Court House as Guardian to Miss Sally
Totty, orphan of Wm. Totty, deceased." Signed, "John
Watkins, Jr."

5 April 1780. WINFREE, William and Ann Chappell, dau. of
James Chappell, who consents. Wit. to consent, Miles
Chappell and John Alex. Pryor. Sur. Miles Chappell.
p. W-2

22 May 1788. WINGO, Abner and Elizabeth Seay, dau. of
Gideon Seay, who consents. Wit. to consent, Thomas Seay
and ____ Seay. Sur. Waller Ford. p. W-3

20 December 1808. WINGO, Allen and Martha Hurt, dau. of
Anson Hurt, who consents. Wit. to consent, Fanny Townes
and George P. Robinson. Sur. George P. Raiborne. Married 22 December by Rev. John Pollard. p. W-5-b

17 December 1788. WINGO, Churchill and Mary Seay, who
writes her own consent. Wit. to consent, Reuben Seay,
James Seay and John Wingo, Senr. Sur. Rawley Fossett.
p. W-3

9 April 1804. WINGO, Fielding and Nancy Willson, who
writes her own consent. Wit. to consent, William Barding
and Lucy Wilson. Sur. William Barding. Married 12 April
by Rev. John Skurrey. p. W-5-a

18 November 1807. WINGO, Henry and Sally W. Baldwin,
dau. of George Baldwin, who consents. Wit. to consent,
W. A. Baldwin and Ann Baldwin. Sur. W. A. Baldwin. Married 19 November by Rev. John Skurrey. p. W-4

18 May 1780. WINGO, John and Frances Seay. Sur. Archer
Cheatham. p. W-2

9 December 1786. WINGO, John and Mary Seay, who writes
her own consent. Wit. to consent, William Wingo and Abner
Wingo. Sur. William Wingo. p. W-3

8 August 1810. WINGO, Joshua A. and Mary Sadler, dau. of
Robert Sadler, who consents. Wit. to consent, John
Booker and Benj. Seay. Sur. John Booker, Jr. Married 10
August by Rev. John Pollard. p. W-5-b

7 September 1784. WINGO, Obediah and Oney Seay, dau. of
Jesse Seay, who consents. Wit. to consent, Gibson Seay
and Larkin Ferguson. Sur. Larkin Ferguson. p. W-3

23 November 1783. WINGO, William and Mary Holt, who
writes her own consent. Sur. John Foster. p. W-2

9 December 1786. WINGO, William and Lurany Loving, dau.
of William Loving, who consents. Wit. to consent, John
Wingo and Abner Wingo. Sur. John Wingo. p. W-3

22 December 1791. WINGO, Zachariah and Sarah Fossit.
Joshua Chaffin's request for this license says, "my
daughter." Sur. Robert Ferguson. John Wingo consents
for son, Zachariah. Wit. to his consent, Sam Jones and
W. T. Townes. p. W-4

1 November 1783. WINN, John and Mary Williams, dau. of
Thomas Williams, whose consent is witnessed by Martha
Greenhill and Wm. Williams. Sur. Wood Jones. p. W-2

12 April 1779. WINN, Richard and Jane Pincham. Rich'd
C. Dennis' request for this license says, "Capt. Winn."
Sur. Chas. Irby. p. W-2

-- ----- ----. WINSTON, Peter and Prudence Scott. Married by Rev. John Finney. Returned to June Court 1791.
Minister's Return.

8 December 1802. WINSTON, Peter and Nancy Crawley Jones,
dau. of John Jones, whose consent says Peter Winston is
of Henrico County. Wit. to consent, David C. Jones and
Mary Jones. Sur. David C. Jones. p. W-5-b

23 December 1811. WOOD, Henry and Martha Murry, who writes her own consent. Wit. to consent, Ann Murry, Frederick Jones and Samuel Greenhill. This is consent ONLY.

2 March 1814. WOOD, Jones and Sally Anderson, dau. of Francis Anderson. Sur. Thomas Pride. Married 3 March by Rev. John Skurrey. p. W-5-b
(Is this a double wedding? See Thomas Pride.)

22 December 1803. WOOD, Thomas D. and Jincey Foster, dau. of Claiborne Foster, who is surety. Married 22 December by Rev. John Pollard. p. W-5-a

-- January 1791. WOOD, Joshua and Polly Carpenter, dau. of Benj. Carpenter, who consents. This is consent ONLY.

25 January 1787. WOOD, William and Susanna Overstreet, dau. of Thos. Overstreet, who consents. Wit. to consent, Robt. Crute and Sharp Lamkin. Sur. Robt. Crute. Married by Rev. Simeon Walton. p. W-3

2 July 1788. WOOD, William and Jane Stern Jeter, dau. of Ambrose Jeter, who consents. Wit. to consent, Henry Haskew and William Crowder. Sur. William Crowder. p. W-3

19 November 1807. WOODSON, Joseph and Sarah M. Booker. Her Guardian, Moses Overton, consents. His consent says Joseph Woodson, Jr. Wit. to consent, Edward Atkinson and Edith C. Booker. Sur. Edward Atkinson. Married 23 November by Rev. Thomas Pettus. p. W-5-a

29 February 1807. WOODSON, Thomas and Martha M. Clements, who writes her own consent. Wit. to consent, John Wingo, Jr. Sur. John Wingo. Jesse Woodson, Guardian of Thomas, consents and says Thomas is son of Hughes Woodson, deceased. Wit. to his consent, John Wingo, Jr. and Hughes Owen. p. W-5-a

20 July 1779. WOODWARD, Jesse and Martha Mayes, who writes her own consent. Sur. Samuel Morgan. p. W-2

13 July 1808. WOODWARD, Thomas and Dorcas Allen, dau. of William Allen, who consents. Wit. to consent, John Allen, who is surety. Wit. to bond, Bentley Anderson. p. W-5-b

25 July 1791. WOOLRIDGE, Daniel and Agnes Osborne. Sur. Abraham Marshall. p. W-4

-- ----- ----. WOOLRIDGE, Spencer and Martha Walke, dau. of H. Walke, whose consent is dated 23 April 1808. Wit. to consent, A. Royall and Page P. Finney. Sur. Page P. Finney. p. W-5-a

124

7 May 1789. WOOSLEY, Moses and Elizabeth Butler. Sur.
William Butler. p. W-4

17 December 1804. WORSHAM, Daniel and Mary Finney, dau.
of Hannah Walke, who consents for "My daughter, Mary Finney." Wit. to consent, W. Finney and Page P. Finney.
William Finney writes request for this license. Sur.
Page P. Finney. p. W-4   (NOTE: Bond and consent are
dated 17 December 1804.)

28 December 1786. WORSHAM, Essex and Elizabeth Dunnavant. Sur. Hodges Dunnavant. Married by Rev. John
Brunskill. p. W-3

11 March 1786. WORSHAM, James and Mary Walthall, dau.
of Dan. Walthall, who consents. Wit. to consent, William Ford and Charles Worsham. Sur. Charles Worsham.
p. W-3

20 April 1794. WORSHAM, John and Nancy Whitworth, Sur.
Charles Worsham. Married by Rev. James McGlasson.
p. W-5-a

21 February 1801. WORSHAM, John and Mary Crittington,
who writes her own consent, witnessed by James Townes,
Clk. Sur. Thomas Dunnavant. p. W-4

23 October 1788. WORSHAM, Thomas and Prudence Gooch.
Sur. William B. Giles. p. W-3

26 March 1801. WORSHAM, Thomas and Patsy Chandler. Sur.
Martin Chandler. Married 8 May by Rev. Walthall Robertson. p. W-4

22 November 1799. WORSHAM, William and Elizabeth Boles,
dau. of Henry Boles, who consents. Wit. to consent, Wm.
Wms. Hall and John Hall. Sur. John Hall. Married 22
November by Rev. Walthall Robertson. p. W-5-a

23 April 1795. WRAY, Thomas and Louisa Howell, whose
Guardian, Abraham Howell, consents. He says, "A
niece of mine, having no parents and lives with me and
I act as Guardian." Wit. to consent, John Hendrick,
Senr., Amey Howell and Edward Hudson. Sur. John Hen-
drick. Married 25 April by Rev. James McGlasson. p. W-4

28 February 1803. WRIGHT, James and Lucy Claiborne.
Sur. James Claiborne. p. W-5-a

16 January 1805. WRIGHT, John and Letitia Pollard. Sur.
Thomas Pollard. Married 17 January by Rev. John Pollard.
p. W-5-a

13 September 1811. WRIGHT, Levi and Elizabeth Furgurson,
dau. of Robert Furgurson, who consents. Wit. to consent,
John Jeter, Wm. T. Crenshaw and James Furgurson. Sur. Wm.
T. Crenshaw. p. W-5-b

23 January 1800. WRIGHT, Pleasant and Sally Mayes. Sur.
Claiborne Foster. Married by Rev. John Pollard. p. W-4

23 July 1789. WRIGHT, Rubin and Polly Foster. William
Wood, Polly's grandfather, in his consent, says Reuben
Wright. Wit. to consent, William Crowder and Henry Haskew. Sur. William Wood, Jr. Married by Rev. John Pollard. p. W-4

17 May 1803. WRIGHT, Samuel and Susannah Pollard, dau.
of Thomas Pollard, who consents. Wit. to consent, Wm.
Wright and George Wright. Sur. Wm. Wright. Wit. to
bond, John T. Leigh and Charles Cocke. Married 18 May by
Rev. John Pollard. p. W-5-b

30 November 1761. WRIGHT, Thomas, Jr. and Edith Hawkins.
Sur. Benjamin Hawkins. p. W-1

22 December 1801. WRIGHT, William and Keturah Wright,
dau. of Thomas Wright, Junr., who consents. Wit. to consent, Nicholas Vaughan and Pleasant Wright. Sur. Pleasant Wright. Married 24 December by Rev. John Pollard.
p. W-5-b

15 June 1790. WYATT, Wm. and Susan Jones. Sur. Peter
Jones. Married by Rev. John Finney. p. W-4

27 December 1764. WYNN, John and Mary Lewis, dau. of
Geo. Lewis, who consents. Sur. Jesse Lunsford. p. W-1

7 December 1786. YOUNG, Leonard and Mary Nance. Sur.
Giles Nance. George and Susanna Young consent. Wit. to
consent, George Reynolds and William Mitchell. Married
by Rev. Simeon Walton. p. Y-1

25 February 1789. YOUNG, Thomas and Elizabeth Nance.
Mary Scales' consent says, "my daughter, Elizabeth Nance."
Wit. to consent, Ellick Moore and David Crenshaw. Sur.
Robert Crute. p. Y-1

27 June 1787. ZACHARY, Crawford and Catrin Gunn, dau. of
James Gunn, who consents. NOTE: "I, Calvin Gunn, agree
to above granted by her father." This note is dated 25
June 1787. Wit. to each consent, Alexander Erskine and
Wm. Gunn. Sur. Alexander Erskine. This bond is on
lower half of p. Y-1

AMELIA COUNTY, VIRGINIA, MARRIAGE BONDS AND

MINISTERS' RETURNS 1744 - 1785

(Accession Number 20920 Virginia State Library)

1.   -- June 1744, JONES, Richard and Elizabeth Jones. Sur: Wm Watson.

2.   25 August 1747, COVINGTON, William and Mary Walker, dau. of Edmund Walker.

3.   19 May 1749, OSBORN, Joseph and Ann Jones.

4.   18 May 1750, MORTON, John and Mary Anderson. Sur: Charles Anderson

5.   7 October 1751, STITH, Buckner and Susanna Munford. Sur: Geo. Walker.

6.   6 August 1753, HARDAWAY, Joseph and Ann Hall, dau. of Jno Hall.
     Sur: Stith Hardaway.

7.   4 April 1754, WINN, John (Gent.) and Susan (Green) Sur: Abraham Green.

8.   15 April 1754, SMITH, George and Ann Smith, widow. Sur: Will. Smith.

9.   21 May 1754, PRYOR, John and Mary Dennis. Sur: Richard Dennis.

10. 22 August 1754, BATT, Chamberlain and Margaret Jones. Sur: Peter Jones.

12. 3 August 1751 (1791)*), HATCHER, Robert and Ann Sanders. * This bond is in
     a very poor state of preservation; someone has written the date and name on
     it, however, the year could be 1791 rather than 1751.

14. 6 October 1762, DENNIS, Henry and Jane Haskins.

15. 4 December 1764, COOKE, Stephen and Amy Jones.

15. 28 June 1765, CHAPPEL, Robert and Sarah Hurt.

16. ------- 1785, ROBERTSON, Nathaniel and Anne Morris.

16. ------- 1785, WESTBROOK, Amos and Elizabeth Palmer.

16. ------- 1785, CABINESS, Elijah and Patty Anthony.

16. ------- 1785, HARRISON, John and Sally Knight.

16. ------- 1785, HAMPTON, John and Joyce Holt.

16. ------- 1785, HARPER, William and Frances Kersey.

NOTE: The marriages are numbered to correspond with numbers in the Accession File
       at Virginia State Library and are not included in Mrs. Williams' book of
       marriages.

Copied by: Emma Robertson Matheny

I N D E X T O B R I D E S

Bass, Elizabeth	18	Bonner, Ann	25
Frances	44	Booker, Ann 53, 60,	98
Mary	10	Ann D.	13
Nancy	95	Caroline	97
Tabitha	44	Edith	14
Bates, Lucy	109	Eliza	22
Sally	109	Elizabeth 56,	97
Baugh, Martha	37	Frances 26,	53
Beacham, Betsy	69	Grace	112
Beadle, Mary	67	Gracy	40
Beaseley, Ann	25	Hannah	11
Bedel, Sarah	59	Jane Davis	17
Belcher, Judith	22	Jean	56
Keziah	22	Judith 12, 37,	57
Mary	34	Kitty	82
Nancy 33,	102	Lucy	25
Prinsey	71	Martha 42,	105
Bell, Anne	78	Mary 24,	78
Betsy	62	Mary Hide	82
Bennett, Susanna	67	Mary Marshall	
Bennitt, Ann	116	Parham	52
Bentley, Judith	37	Nancy C.	36
Mary	13	Nancy M.	91
Rachel	96	Purify	50
Berry, Elizabeth	80	Rachel M.	107
Joannah	9	Rachel Marrott	107
Lucy	10	Rebecca	103
Martha Ann	89	Rebecca H.	107
Polly	71	Sally B.	90
Beuford, Catherine	50	Sally M.	97
Bevill, Betsy	18	Sally Marshall	97
Elizabeth	84	Sarah 12,	24
Frances	87	Sarah M.	123
Liza	27	Statira	7
Lucy	27	Booth, Elizabeth	77
Nancy Hill	2	Judith	80
Patsy Tatum	35	Mary	76
Patty	44	Rebecca	15
Polly	60	Boothe, Phebe	12
Ridley	80	Borum, Polly	16
Sarah	79	Bott, Ann	4
Susannah	2	Elizabeth T.	63
Suzaner	2	Martha	16
Tabitha	84	Sarah	16
Blackburn, Sally Anderson	3	Bottom, Frances	27
Bland, Clara	12	Bowles, Page F.	92
Blankenship, Nancy	52	Page Finney	92
Sally L. (?)	14	Bowman, Mary	40
Boggess, Hannah	50	Polley	72
Boles, Elizabeth	124	Bracket, Nancy	53
Bolling, Frances	74	Brackett, Ann	6
Mary T.	103	Ann H.	51

Brackett, Ann Harris	51	Cardwell, Patsey	1
Flizabeth P.	50	Carpenter, Jane	9
Judith A.	56	Jenny	9
Judith W.	11	Patty	55
Sally	102	Polly	123
Bradley, Polly	45	Sally	111
Branch, Obedience	118	Carter, Betsy F.	100
Ridley	120	Phebe	61
Susanna I.	65	Cavender, Betsy	28
Braughton, Elizabeth	45	Sally	28
Braxenian (?), Usle	21	Chaffin, Betse	42
Brewer, Elizabeth 70,	96	Jinney	61
Bridgforth, Elizabeth	71	Nancy	97
Bridgewater, Prudence	99	Chandler, Lucy	9
Broadnax, Ann	79	Nancy	89
Brogan (?), Agnes	105	Patsy	124
Brooking, Ann	17	Chapman, Jane	115
Elizabeth B.	72	Jean	115
Elizabeth T.	53	Mahala	86
Frances 17,	91	Nancy	28
Frances V.	17	Sally White	115
Sarah	24	Chappell, Ann	121
Brooks, Ann	116	Catherine	65
Frances	40	Doretha	101
Winny	16	Dorothy	101
Brown, Elizabeth	107	Elizabeth	29
Janet	49	Martha 56,	110
Lucretia	44	Patty	105
Mary	79	Sarah 26,	41
Bruice, Prudence	56	Cheatham, Sally	71
Bryan, Susanna	62	Claiborne, Catharine	55
Buford, Catherine	50	Lucy	124
Burton, Frances	31	Mary	104
Judith	78	Nancy	21
Martha	113	Clardy, Milly	20
Butler, Elizabeth	124	Sally	54
Martha	60	Sarah	20
Nancy	113	Clark, Lucy	80
Polly	19	Clarke, Rachel	120
		Susannah	113
C		Clay, Ann	26
		Cary J. 68,	119
Cabiness, Hannah	25	Dicy	35
Jemima	106	Dolly 1,	6
Cadtington, Prudence Ann	34	Elizabeth	100
Callicott, Clary	15	Elizabeth R.	1
Dicey	17	Martha 11,	26
Prudence	5	Nancy	28
Cannon, Leonia	80	Patsy	100
Levinia	80	Phebe	62
Cardwell, Elizabeth	59	Rhoda	47
Mary	120	Sally	55

INDEX TO SURETIES AND OTHERS

Clay, Charles, Sr.	1	
Daniel	68	
Daniel W.	11, 119	
David	54	
Eleazer	106	
Isham	90	
Jesse	1, 11, 28, 68	
John	1, 26, 62	
Robert	11	
Thomas	35	
Clayborne, Wm.	117	
Claybrook, Edward	46, 62	
Peter	26, 66, 77	
William	77	
Clayton,	114	
Clement, Francis	39	
Susannah H.	46	
Clements, Isham	13,16,19,85	
Joseph	82	
Simon	59	
William	19, 82	
Wm.	16	
Wm., Junr.	117	
Clemons, Anna	108	
John	67, 108, 112	
Cliburn, Leonard	104	
Clough, Eliza	32	
Eliza, Senr.	32	
Richard	84, 110	
Childress, Robert	24	
Cobbs, John C.	12, 27, 75	
	82, 94	
John Catlin	56	
John E.	5	
Sam	52	
Sam'l	1, 3, 13, 14,24	
	79, 101	
Samuel	12, 13, 28	
Sarah	75	
Thomas M.	3	
Cock (?), Wm. May	28	
Cocke, Abraham	31, 49, 67	
Abra:, Jr.	49	
Abraham, Senr.	38	
Batt	99	
Charles	125	
James	37, 102	
James P.	78	
Lee	105	
Stephen	5, 31, 38	
Susanah	46	
Cole, Frances	9	

Coleman, A.	15	
Anderson	26	
Archer	20, 77, 81, 85	
Armistead	1	
Braxton	86	
Burrel	20, 31	
Burwell	1,27,31, 51, 81	
Cain	84	
Daniel	16, 26, 28, 51	
	76, 104	
Daniel, Jr.	16	
Daniel, Senr.	16	
Ebenezer	100	
Eleazer	35	
Elizabeth	11	
Elizabeth, Sr.	84	
Fatha	16	
Isaac	28	
James	11	
Jesse	2, 18, 66	
Jos:	87	
Laban	111	
Martha	16	
Moses	17	
Robert	24	
Sarah	2	
Solomon	10, 84	
William	11, 26, 44, 86	
Collie, John	13	
Compton, Elizabeth	117	
Jeremiah	28	
Joel	115	
Zachariah	39	
Cook, James	29, 77, 79	
John	95	
Joseph	1	
Stephen	21	
Cooke, Batte	119	
James	6	
Raines	19	
Cooper, Edmund	29	
John L.	5, 29, 34	
Cordle, Elizabeth	74	
Richd	74	
Cousins, Charles A.	121	
Elizabeth	19	
John	72, 104, 121	
John C.	6, 19	
Robert	19, 64	
William	24, 64	
Covington, George	96	
Cox, Henry	15	

* * * * * * * * * * * * * * * *